# Learning Centre

Park Road, Uxbridge Middlesex UB8 1NQ
Renewals: 01895 853326 Enquiries: 01895 853344

Please return this item to the Learning Centre on or before this last date
stamped below:

| | | |
|---|---|---|
| | | |

301

## SHORT INTRODUCTIONS

**Published**

Nicholas Abercrombie, *Sociology*
Robert W. Connell, *Gender*
Stephanie Lawson, *International Relations*

**Forthcoming**

Mike Bury, *Health*
Peter Dear and H. M. Collins, *Science*
Loraine Gelsthorpe, *Criminology*
Colin Hay, *Politics*
Christina Toren, *Anthropology*

# Sociology

Nicholas Abercrombie

polity

First published in 2004 by Polity Press Ltd.

Reprinted 2004, 2005

Polity Press
65 Bridge Street
Cambridge CB2 1UR, UK

Polity Press
350 Main Street
Malden, MA 02148, USA

A catalogue record for this book is available from the British Library.

**Library of Congress Cataloging-in-Publication Data**

Abercrombie, Nicholas.
   Sociology / Nicholas Abercrombie.
      p. cm. – (Short introductions)
   Includes bibliographical references and index.
      ISBN 0-7456-2541-X (hb : alk. paper) – ISBN 0-7456-2542-8 (pb : alk. paper)
   1. Sociology.   I. Title.   II. Series.
   HM585.A243 2004
   301 – dc21                                               2003014195

Typeset in 10 on 12 pt Sabon
by SNP Best-set Typesetter Ltd., Hong Kong
Printed and bound in Great Britain by TJ International, Padstow, Cornwall

For further information on Polity, visit our website: www.polity.co.uk

# Contents

Acknowledgements                                        vii
Preface                                                 ix

1  The reality of everyday life                          1

2  Who do we think we are?                               6
   Jazz and hash                                         7
   The social construction of identity                   8
   Identity and belonging                               10
   Identity as difference                               16
   Identity and social change                           18

3  Who do we love?                                      22
   Intimacy and romance                                 22
   Intimacy and partnership                             27
   Private love                                         29
   Friendship                                           33
   The self                                             34

4  Who do we talk to?                                   38
   The wider family                                     41
   Local communities and neighbours                     43
   Associations                                         47
   Social networks and social health                    50

5   Is work a curse?                                55
      What is work?                                 56
      The organization of work                      58
      Changing work                                 63

6   Does inequality matter?                         72
      Inequality of condition                       74
      Systems of inequality                         79
      Social class                                  80
      Inequality of opportunity                     85

7   Why don't things fall apart?                    89
      The problem of order                          89
      Coercion                                      92
      Common values                                 98
      Altruism, exchange and trust                 101

8   Has the magic gone?                            106
      Measurement and calculation                  107
      Efficiency and control                       111
      Moral decline and disenchantment             115

9   What can sociology do for you?                 120

Notes                                             125
Index                                             136

# Acknowledgements

A large number of people have helped with the writing of this book. I am very grateful to: colleagues who generously took over some of my responsibilities while I was writing   Colin Adams, Mandy Chetwynd, Tessa Harrison, Ray Macdonald, Chris Park, Lesley Wareing and Nigel Whiteley; Polity's anonymous readers for their initial suggestions on my proposal and then for not making too many on the final draft; academic colleagues who have patiently answered my uninformed questions about sources, ideas or data – Susan Condor, Bob Jessop, Charlie Lewis, Andrew Sayer and Jackie Stacey; friends – Brian Longhurst, John Urry and Alan Warde – who have been sources of ideas and inspiration over far too many years, and have now been rewarded by being asked to read the whole manuscript in draft; Polity staff, especially Louise Knight and Caroline Richmond, who have again shown how efficient, helpful and tolerant publishers can be; Bren Abercrombie, Joe Abercrombie and Rob Abercrombie, who read the whole text, made detailed comments, told me about books, films and television programmes, and were willing to talk about sociology at any time of day or night.

For Rob and Joe Abercrombie

# Preface

I work in a university sociology department. Like most people, I am fre-quently asked what I do for a living. In asking that question, people do not expect a catalogue of sociological findings or, at least, they would soon glaze over if that was the response that they got. Rather, they want to know what it is *like* to teach and research in sociology. This book is an attempt to answer that question. In writing it, I have shied away from the textbook approach designed for students taking particular courses and with a content dictated by the way that professional sociologists divide up their subject. Instead, I have aimed at a rather more diverse audience, including existing students and professionals of the subject, people who are wondering whether to take up sociology in some way and that most elusive of creatures, the general reader. This book tries to describe what it is like to do sociology, how sociologists think, and what is distinctive about the sociological habit of mind.

As far as I am concerned, the most significant example of the genre in which I am writing remains Peter Berger's *Invitation to Sociology*.[1] Although this fair, challenging and, above all, humane book is now forty years old, it still has the power to draw people to sociology as well as to impress cynical professors of the subject. It is also a *systematic* book in that it adopts a particular approach to the subject that links together the separate chapters. I share Berger's aim to invite the reader to an intel-lectual world that is profoundly exciting and significant, but I have chosen to take a different tack in realizing this aim. Rather than taking an analytical or theoretical approach to the qualities of mind that are distinctive to the sociological enterprise, I have chosen to try to *illustrate* them by showing how sociologists tackle particular problems that relate directly to people's lives. My purpose is to intrigue the reader, to draw him or her in, by treating a set of questions that I believe are interesting and which I know have interested others. The book is organized into chapters, each of which is a discussion of a question that anybody might well ask themselves. In adopting this method, I have tried to vary the pace of discussion, giving detailed accounts of particular studies that seem to me to be successful while going fairly quickly over other areas.

One result of this approach is that I am not aiming at complete coverage of the subject or even of individual topics. As I have said, this is not a textbook, and some important sociological topics and arguments will inevitably be left out. Readers who are looking for greater depth on any issue may follow up the reading mentioned in the notes. In addition, the limited space available, combined with the decision to concentrate on a small number of topics in some detail, means that I have not been able to take illustrations from a wide variety of societies. Most of my examples, therefore, are inevitably based on American and British sources. Another consequence is that I may well disappoint some of my professional colleagues. I have not made a particular line or approach prominent in the discussion. There are arguments that run through the book – about the naturalness of the everyday world or about sociology as a moral enterprise, for example – but I have not wanted them to drive its organization. In addition, the reader will find very little on such staples as the history of the subject, detailed accounts of the work of particular sociologists, methods of social inquiry, or sociological theory. Rather, I have wanted to show what sociologists can say about questions that are both important and interesting and how their analyses can illuminate and enrich the conduct of everyday life to everybody's benefit.

Nick Abercrombie
Lancaster, May 2003

# The reality of everyday life

Without the aid of prejudice and custom, I should not be able to find my way across the room.

William Hazlitt

The Wenhaston family is getting up to begin the working day. The parents, Alison and David, are almost always up first. Sophie, the younger child, is next and Tom, who is fifteen and unable to find his school tie, is inevitably last down to breakfast. The meal is rushed and everybody is soon out of the house. Sophie, who is eight, is taken to school by David, who then goes on to his work as a technician with a company manufacturing specialized computer systems. Alison drives herself to the offices of the insurance company where she is a claims supervisor. Tom meets a group of friends outside the local McDonald's and goes on to school by bus.

The working day passes quickly, mostly because it is rushed. A couple of Alison's staff are off sick and she has to arrange cover for them, which consists largely in dealing with customers herself. As far as David can see, there are never enough staff to sort out technical problems in his company. The school day drags a little more but, for both Sophie and Tom, the experience is improved by being able to talk to their friends. Tom, in particular, is looking forward to the evening as he is going out to a club where a band from the school is playing.

Since it is a Friday and not followed by a school day, Alison and David are not unduly concerned about Tom's clubbing, although they worry about the possibility of drug-taking, but they do expect him to be back at home no later than one o'clock. Unexpectedly, Sophie's best friend has asked her to spend the weekend at her house and, excited, Sophie rushes off as soon as she can. As a result, Alison and David find themselves with an evening free of children. Alison wonders whether to go and see her parents who live a little bit less than an hour's drive away. However, she is tired by the day's work and decides, a little guiltily, not to do so. In addition, she has some washing and ironing to do. Although David is very good at helping her with the housework, she still finds that she does the bulk of it in addition to working full-time. Alison's decision not to visit her parents influences David's decision not to go to a meeting at the local community centre about the growth in local traffic. They both settle down in front of the television after a hurried evening meal and Tom finds them still there when he comes in.

This is a simple description of an ordinary day that would be perfectly recognizable to a large proportion of the population. As a rule, people go through the day without asking profound questions about their own conduct. They do not, therefore, wonder all day whether their behaviour is typical of the population at large, why they hold the beliefs that they do, or how their own behaviour influences that of their children. It is this apparently unquestioning quality of everyday life that intrigues or infuriates creators of fiction. For every character bar one in the film *Groundhog Day*, for instance, every day is exactly the same as the one before. Only the hero knows this. For everyone else, it is as if they started the day anew with no memory of previous events. The result is that everyday life is entirely unquestioned; the characters have no vantage point outside the everyday which would give an alternative perspective.

Of course, from time to time, particular circumstances may force people to reflect on their own lives. A row over who should do the washing up, for example, might prompt Alison and David to ask themselves how it is that men and women share out the housework in the way that they do and what justifies the distribution that they adopt. The very fact that everyday life is organized into provinces[1] may make us more self-reflective. Thus, everyday life at home, at work, or with friends is all very different. These are separate provinces which can be used to give a more distant perspective on one another. For example, the fact that Alison is treated as an important person at work may make her resent the way she is treated at home by her husband and children. More extensively still, serious illness or holidays may make the routines of everyday life seem precarious or drab. Great public events also have the effect of making us stop and think. For example, many people said, at the time, that the death of Princess Diana changed their lives. It is true that they will probably think otherwise now, since such events are a bit like fireworks; they have powerful effects at the time but then die away all too quickly. All of these circumstances disrupt our everyday world temporarily and make us aware of the routine that is characteristically hidden.

Even more radically, people occasionally go through life-changing events that make their lives extraordinary for a time. Falling in love or religious conversion are examples of such changes. Very few people, however, live truly extraordinary lives all the time so that each day is different from the one before. For most people, most of the time, everyday life is simply *there*; it is an overwhelming fact of life and any disruptions to it are merely temporary. People's energies are focused on getting through the day, and, to do that, it is necessary to take the world around us for granted rather than to question it. There is, furthermore, a very important reason why people should avoid looking into their everyday lives too directly. Everyday life is a very significant source of *security*. People gain their sense of life's solidity precisely from their unvarying routine – going to work and coming home again, eating meals with the family, watching the television. There are limits to the extent that questioning and upsetting everyday life is psychologically tolerable.[2]

Despite the relative solidity, security and generally unquestioned nature of everyday life, the description of the Wenhastons' day does raise a multitude of sociological questions. For example, are Alison and David's fears about drug-taking a realistic assessment of the risks that Tom runs? Why is it that Alison is seeing her parents less as the years go by, and is she alone in that? How does Tom fit in with his friends? Why is David paid more than Alison? Has the pace of their working lives increased? Why is there such a gap in age between Sophie and Tom? Is the marital relationship between Alison and David characteristic of the twenty-first century? Will Sophie and Tom replicate the relationships of their parents? Why is the world around the Wenhastons reasonably ordered and regular?

Now, of course, one does not have to be a sociologist to ask these questions or to propose a few answers. They are, on the face of it, commonsense questions which could have, and do receive, commonsense answers. Many sociologists would like to think that this is because sociological thinking has become widespread and is influential in the media and public debate, and even in everyday conversation. This clearly is true to some extent. Thus, standard sociological ideas such as globalization or individualization, which will be discussed later on in this book, are frequently aired by newspapers or politicians. But it is more likely to be because such questions deal with the familiar world of everyday, and people will feel that, in this arena, they are experts and they have the capacity and experience to ask and answer them. This is not the world of particle physics or microbiology which are realms where the unqualified might well fear to tread. If provoked, anyone can have an opinion about society.

The subject matter of sociology therefore creates a potential difficulty for sociologists. Because they deal with questions on which everyone can have an opinion, they can be accused of stating the obvious. The saying that the sociologist is someone who spends a million dollars to find his way to the whorehouse encapsulates that view. Actually, there is nothing wrong in investigating an issue in social life, gathering evidence and coming up with conclusions that seem perfectly obvious. We need to be sure, after all, that even obvious judgements are well supported by evidence. There is, however, a more serious point about the relationship between sociology and commonsense.

Our commonsense judgements may deceive. This is for two reasons. I have already pointed out that our everyday world, and the commonsense that goes with it, is very powerful. The world that we inhabit seems to be the only one that there is. It is the paramount reality. Such a view is confirmed by the information that we receive. Although we may appear to be bombarded by information about other ways of living from across the world, actually most of us do not come into contact with these alternatives at all regularly or profoundly. Our everyday lives, which are conducted in a fairly limited circle, are therefore self-confirming. It is a world of stereotypes and of 'what everybody knows'. This feature is, of course, fundamental to the frequent conflicts, in Northern Ireland or Palestine, for instance, that occur between different social groups, each of which has an everyday life which seems to them to be the only one. They literally do not understand each other. In fact, our larger social world has infinite variety, and it is the sociologist's task to understand that variety.[3]

The commonsense of our everyday lives misleads for a more fundamental reason, however. Because we take our everyday world for granted – it is simply *there* – we do not typically question it or ask *why* it takes the form that it does. In a sense, therefore, everyday life obscures its own conditions of production, obscures the social factors that have produced it. Sociology attempts to understand those conditions and to see each specific social situation as an example of a general type. One way in which this can happen is by comparing one everyday reality with another. For example, in the next chapter I will be describing the social structure of a group of punks. For the people concerned, their lives form a self-confirming whole which, to them, is special and unusual. However, this punk group is very like other youth cultures in its social structure. Furthermore, it is very like apparently profoundly different social groups such as those that form round a hobby of some kind or which adopt extreme political or religious beliefs. All these groups have a hierarchy of prestige. Those with the greatest prestige form a core who are the most 'authentic', wholeheartedly adopting the way of life concerned.

These comparisons between sociological and commonsense reasoning show how disruptive sociology can be. Far from stating the merely obvious, the discipline challenges many of the assumptions on which our everyday lives are based. Those challenges can make people angry or surprised or intrigued or transformed – or even reassured. I will be giving examples of these responses in the pages that follow. They can also call into question official accounts. For example, it had long been thought that the unemployed were a section of the community more or less permanently in that state, through absence of local employment opportunities, lack of skill and education, or weakness of motivation. Government social policy was therefore organized towards the idea of long-term employment with measures designed to tackle lack of employment opportunities or to improve individual motivation or skill. Sociological research, on the other hand, has shown that a substantial proportion of the unemployed population are only without work temporarily and may move in and out of that state.[4] Many people will experience a period of unemployment at some time in their lives. Such a conclusion suggests quite different social policies. It also, incidentally, may help to reassure those who do become unemployed. They are not somehow deficient as members of a sub-class but are much like many others, many of whom will find work again.

Sociology, therefore, does not promote *discovery* in the same sense as the natural sciences do. It does not produce the equivalent of a new galaxy or a new bacterium. But it *is* like the natural sciences in that it is curious about the world and does not take it for granted. It tries to identify and solve the puzzles that the social world throws up and, in doing so, provides the way of giving a different meaning to the cosy, everyday world around us. The chapters that follow illustrate how sociology addresses some of these puzzles.

# 2

# Who do we think we are?

I don't want to belong to any club that will accept me as a member.
Groucho Marx

In the last chapter I noted that, typically, we take our everyday world for granted. We do not, on the whole, question it. For example, we do not worry significantly about our identity – about who we are or which of our qualities are really important to us. It is true that, at particular moments in a person's life, such questions may surface. At retirement, for instance, people may look forward to a rest, but they may also reflect on what it will be like not to be a person who works at such and such a job. Similarly, a woman who has had a break from work to have children but is wondering whether to return to work may worry whether she can cope with being a career woman rather than a mother. People who are retiring or who are re-entering the labour market are clearly altering some crucial aspect of their identity. Again, it is equally important for us to be able to *place* others, to know how they fit in, because that will tell us what kind of person they are. So, if a student arriving at university for the first time is introduced to someone new, it is likely that both will ask where home is and what their parents do for a living, and they will try to discover each other's tastes in music, film or books. Other signs of identity will be relatively obvious – gender, ethnicity, clothing and appearance, or age, for example. These tactics of personal interaction are important to the conduct of social life, even if they are carried out largely without anyone's being aware of it. So, how is identity created, maintained and changed?

## Jazz and hash

The beginning of an answer to this question can be found in two studies by Howard Becker, one of dance musicians and the other of marihuana users, mostly carried out in Chicago in the 1950s.[1] For most of the musicians that Becker interviewed, music, particularly jazz, formed an important, if not *the* most important, part of their lives. Their personal identities were formed by their activities as jazz musicians. In the creation and maintenance of that identity, Becker points to the significance of a self-conception as an artist, the manner in which musicians react to their audience, and the way that the culture of musicians functions. A substantial part of the self-esteem of Becker's musicians was derived from their view of themselves as players of jazz as distinct from commercial music. Unfortunately, their audiences – and the musicians interviewed by Becker played in clubs, bars and dance-halls, at weddings and birthdays, and on the radio – did not especially like jazz and wanted their celebrations and evenings out to be accompanied by something that they could dance to. The musicians therefore were caught in a contradiction. They could persist with their self-conception as artists, playing what they saw as proper music and earn very little money, or they could play music liked by their audiences and have something to live on. Whatever the response, however, all the musicians continued to believe that the right thing to do would be to play jazz, to be artists, even if circumstances conspired to force them to do otherwise.

The fact that audiences wanted to listen to one kind of music but the musicians wanted to play another is related to the relationship between the two. Musicians held the audience in contempt. Interestingly, Becker notes that this is often true of the relationship between the provider of a service and its recipient. For the former the latter is at best an inconvenience and at worst an enemy. It is as if the self-esteem of the provider was at risk by being in a service role and a dismissive attitude to the client or customer is some kind of protection.

The musicians formed a self-segregated group with its own culture and ways of behaving. They associated only with each other not least because their hours and places of working did not fit in with mainstream life. Their everyday life was underpinned by the very language that they used, and their conversation was peppered by expressions which only they could understand. Importantly also, the group was the means by which musicians got work. In a system of mutual help, they passed on each other's names to potential employers.

In much the same way that musicians form a distinctive group, so also do marihuana users. Becker's interest is in how people learn to use the drug, and it is worth remembering that the research was conducted in the 1950s when attitudes to marihuana were very different. He shows how new users first have to learn the technique of smoking effectively. They then have to perceive the effects as the effects of the drug. Lastly, those effects have to be seen as enjoyable. It is not, in other words, that one can become an accomplished user easily because the drug has inevitable effects. People have a great deal to *learn*. And that learning is, of course, essentially a social activity. Here is a user describing his first encounter with marihuana:

> I came on like I had turned on many times before, you know. I didn't want to seem like a punk to this cat. See, I didn't know the first thing about it – how to smoke it, or what was going to happen, or what. I just watched him like a hawk – I didn't take my eyes off him for a second, because I wanted to do everything just as he did it.[2]

These two studies may be of unusual identities formed and sustained by unusual groups, but they do raise questions about identity in general. First, they suggest that identity is socially constructed. It is not some fixed or innate quality but is created and then changed in interaction with others. Second, identity is wrapped up with a sense of belonging. Intrinsic to knowing who you are is a felt membership in a social group or groups comprised of people who are similar. Third, identity is also a question of difference. Part of my knowing who I am is knowing who I am not. Fourth, because identity is acquired – learned – it is malleable, and it is more malleable in some societies than others. For example, people living in modern societies may have a more fragmented and fast-changing sense of identity than those living in, say, nineteenth-century Japan.

## The social construction of identity

Commonsensically, we think of our identities as fixed and pretty well established. We carry them around as a kind of nut inside us. So, I am male, white, British, born and bred in London, with a whole range of likes and dislikes. Furthermore, to the extent that we think about it at all, we tend to think of these features of identity as biologically rooted or acquired in early infancy. True, we may believe that other, less important, aspects of identity are picked up in later life. Perhaps we will also think that everybody has a tendency to behave differently in different circumstances. For example, someone brought up in a household in Surrey will develop an accent to match. But when placed in different company, at university in Lancashire perhaps, that accent will change to fit in better with the new social environment. However significant these later acquisitions of marks of identity, we still tend to see them as unimportant compared with the inner self, the true or authentic self. And note how important the idea of authenticity is in everyday life. A change in accent, the adoption of different attitudes or a rejection of a parent's taste are often seen as hypocrisy, social climbing or a betrayal of the true, inner self formed in early life. Furthermore, this idea of the authentic, natural self is what makes it so very difficult to understand apparent sudden changes of identity, following an accident, for example, or as in religious conversion, of which more in a moment.

In everyday life, then, we tend to think of identity as fairly fixed and established in early childhood. Sociology, on the other hand, thinks of identity as very much more plastic and variable and formed by social relationships with others. Such an account implies that our sense of who we are is constructed out of an engagement between our view of our own identity and others' view of it. In a multitude of ways a father may, generally without realizing it, project to his son a view of what it takes to be a man. In talking about school, he will stress the importance of standing up for oneself. He will make it clear that sport is a masculine preserve in which one plays to win. At home, the father's behaviour will indicate what domestic tasks are to be performed by women and what by men. But the son's masculinity does not emerge fully formed from this encounter alone. Others will have a role – his mother, teachers, friends. Furthermore, this is a continuous process whereby, throughout his life, the boy refines and develops his sense of manhood by means of his relationships with others. Identity, in sum, is a *negotiation*.

An extreme version of this sociological account is that identity is no more than a series of masks put on for each social encounter. There is no real or authentic inner self, only a series of performances, which will be different in different circumstances.[3] While such a view is valuable in calling attention to the way in which identity changes over time or between different social situations, it goes too far. Over a person's life, an identity as a particular kind of person is built up, and it is that identity that confronts others' expectations and actions and may resist them. Radical change in adult identity is rare, however much publicity is given to religious conversion, the brainwashing of captured soldiers or those who suffer serious accidents. But it is entirely common for people to change the sense of who they are more slowly as they interact with other people. It is, therefore, foolish to deny that there is a difference between more fundamental features of identity such as gender and rather more trivial aspects such as a taste for television soap opera. There are *primary identities* which are fairly resistant to change. But even here we should be wary of seeing these primary identities as absolutely fixed and *natural*. In contemporary societies, instances of changing gender may receive much publicity, although it is true that they are rare. Nonetheless, men can pass as women (for that is the more common case) with a great deal of success.[4] What such cases show is that any society will have a carefully constructed set of conceptions of what it is to be a woman or a man, and those conceptions seem entirely natural and taken for granted. Any attempt to cross the divide between man and woman can be profoundly upsetting for those who witness it – but it is also very revealing of the way that societies build up stereotypes of gender upon biological differences which could, in fact, justify a whole range of different ways of being a woman or man.[5]

Because women and men have certain biological differences, there is a temptation, therefore, to associate a further set of characteristics with those differences and assume that women *naturally* want to marry, have children, stay at home and generally abstain from participation in the public world. These characteristics, however, are limited to particular times, places and societies; actually there are many different ways of being a woman, and these differences are frequently more important than the basic similarity of being biologically female. The evidence about simple societies gathered by anthropologists shows that women can be warriors, major economic producers, religious functionaries and leaders.[6] In contemporary Western societies, for that matter, the roles played by women are beginning to change, as we shall see later on in this book. What seems perfectly natural to the members of one society may well seem extraordinarily strange to another.

## Identity and belonging

A sense of who we are is inseparable from a feeling of belonging to some social entity larger than we are. This can be an explicit membership. For instance, an important part of a man's identity may come from membership of a 1950s rock-and-roll society. He might be secretary of the society, spend a good part of each week on its business and go on rock-and-roll weekends. Or it might be a sense of belonging to a social group, such as a local community, which is more rarely invoked. In modern societies, local communities may not function extensively as systems of mutual support. But at times of trial, for example, if a factory rendering animal fat and incidentally producing noxious smells is to be built nearby, people do remember what they have in common with their neighbours. Or it might be a membership which is so taken for granted that people never reflect on it, as in the case of gender. In all these instances, however, identity involves a sense of being *like* certain other people who are all members of a collectivity, however loosely defined.

A variety of mechanisms – what one could call *strategies of belonging* – connect up belonging with identity. Many social groups from which people derive part of their identity cultivate a distinctive *visual appearance*. Youth cultures such as punks or skinheads are obvious instances of this. People who see themselves as punks will instantly recognize that others of similar appearance will be like them in other critical respects. Such spectacular marks of membership may be relatively rare. However, more subtle aspects of clothing, hairstyle or make-up give signals of common identity. At a party, for instance, two people may recognize that they are both wearing Armani. That recognition confirms their identity as (expensively) fashion-conscious individuals who are members of a select band. Further, social groups may enforce a conformity of appearance which strengthens the sense of common identity. In some occupations, the military or flight attendants, for example, this is made explicit in the wearing of uniform. But, more commonly, it is subtle. For example, a study of the way that managers operate[7] shows how a dress code works in certain organizations. This code is not promulgated officially or written down. It is just that managers know that they do not wear sports jackets (too informal) or brown suits (a loser's colour); they do not leave their floor without a jacket on; they do not wear casual shoes or suits not made of natural fibres; but they do wear red ties. This knowledge of the appropriate dress that signals membership of the management is reinforced by everyday behaviour. So, those who step out of line are the subject of jokes or, at worst, unfavourable gossip.

These features of appearance act as signals, means of communication. So also, in a rather more obvious way, does *language*. For example, an ex-musician in Becker's study noted how musicians talked differently from other people. To be a musician did not depend solely on being able to play an instrument skilfully. It also involved the ability to use the right slang. And this may extend to names. Within cultures – whether they are based on work, leisure or community – the use of nicknames is widespread. They reinforce the sense of belonging, particularly as they are typically not used outside the group. Similarly, many work cultures have ways of talking, perhaps involving the use of specialized terms or unfamiliar usages of ordinary words, which exclude outsiders but which give a sense of belonging to all those who do understand. The use of particular phrases will spread rapidly through a social group and will act as a sign of acceptance and membership. For instance, managers of all kinds seem to find it impossible to get through the day without using such expressions as 'progress this action', 'issues around this agenda', 'singing from the same hymn-sheet' or 'joined-up thinking', all really to do with the futility of action in any organization. Non-verbal communication can also signal membership. Hand gestures, posture, even a style of walking can all be distinctive in different groups. Again, this can be formal, as in the soldier's tendency to stand to attention even when off duty. But it is more likely to be an unconscious adoption of the habits of those around, as in the slouched posture favoured by some youth cultures. The television series *Faking It* illustrates these points in an interesting way. In these programmes, people who did not have the appropriate skills for a profession were taught them in a few weeks. Thus, a call-centre manager was trained rapidly to become a television director. These amateurs were then placed in a 'real' situation to see if they could pass as professionals when nobody around them knew who they were. A strikingly large number managed to pass this test. But what enabled them to be accepted was only partly that they had the relevant skills. It was also that they talked and dressed just like the professionals.

The use of *symbols* can reinforce belonging. The presence of national flags at football matches or crucifixes at an anti-abortion rally instantly conveys an identity. In England, the St George's cross has become adopted by those who believe that a traditional way of life is threatened. The use of the symbol by road-side snack bars in the country is, perhaps, an indication of what kind of person you may expect to find there having a cup of tea. Of course, it is not the physical object – the flag – that does the symbolic work by itself. It is the associations of ideas that provide the force, and symbols are important because they condense and organize the way that we think. Some politicians become extremely skilled at exploiting the symbolic power of ideas for their own purposes. For example, Churchill and Thatcher used the idea of Britishness as a symbol of identity in trying to unite the country behind particular policies. Symbols only work in constructing and signalling identity because people have powers of *imagination*. Many of the memberships that give us a sense of identity are solid and direct, even organized. If I have joined the local branch of the National Trust or have become a student at the local further education college, there will be rules of membership, formal procedures of admission, and I will personally know many of the people in the same position. With other groups with which I identify, however, there are not so many concrete marks of membership and I have to use my imagination. The identification as a member of a nation is an obvious illustration of this point. The idea of the nation is very powerful and can mobilize a population's energy, loyalty and trust in a way few other institutions can. The nation is also a community in that there is a strong sense of belonging to a common entity and having a shared sentiment, history and purpose. But, however strong the sense of community is in the nation, it is not founded in personal relationships, as are many forms of identity. Each member of the nation-community therefore has to be able to imagine other members. Nations are 'imagined communities'.[8]

Imagination, fantasy and day-dreaming are important, if relatively unrecognized, aspects of our daily lives. They are, in general, ways of maintaining our sense of who we are – and who we might become.[9] Day-dreaming is a speculation about what the future holds, but it is a pleasurable speculation which is distinct from fantasy because it contains elements that are possible and realistic. Individuals may therefore day-dream about a future event, a wedding perhaps, in which their new clothes are perfect, the sun is shining and the wedding march is played perfectly. These speculations are pleasurable in themselves, but there is also pleasure in the knowledge that their realization is perfectly possible.

Day dreaming of this sort can maintain – or change – identity, as reality is brought into line with the dream.[10] It is given a peculiarly modern twist because day-dreaming is so much helped by the omnipresence of the media in modern societies. The media provide large and complex repertoires of images and narratives out of which people construct scripts of imagined lives. Clearly, the media can fuel the imagination in different ways and at different levels. Magazines produce recipes which give rise to the imagined perfection of a dinner party; advertisements for holidays generate dreams of sun, sand and the perfect body; television soap opera exemplifies human relationships which can be an imaginative resource; and films will use stars who provide a means of identification and fantasy.[11]

In an earlier part of this chapter I talked about the theory of identity as a set of masks. Such a conception raises the question as to whether there is a 'real' identity, a real me behind the mask. This question is also one that is asked in everyday life, as in: 'Is he just playing at being a punk or is he really one?' Claims and counter-claims about *authenticity*, in other words, are significant strategies of belonging. A study of a group of American punks meeting regularly in a bar illustrates this point.[12] Within the group, four layers or circles could be distinguished, differentiated from each other by their degree of commitment to the punk culture and therefore by the degree to which they were 'authentically' punk. The inner core set the trends and standards for the group as a whole. They were dedicated to the punk ideal of being resolutely against conventional society, bureaucracy and private property. They did not have full-time employment, living instead on welfare payments or jobs, such as rock musician or actor, that could be seen as consistent with the counter-cultural ideal. Their appearance was important because it set them apart. Their aim was to live life for the moment without regard for future consequences. As a result, their drug-taking habits verged on the self-destructive.

Around this inner ring of authentic punks, who lived the lifestyle, was a larger group less dedicated to the counter-culture. Theirs was a qualified authenticity, and, for that reason, they did not have the prestige attaching to the inner core. They realized, as did the inner core, that their commitment, although strong, was temporary and they would move on to some other definition of identity. They differed from the core, therefore, in that the latter had essentially undergone a process of conversion. A larger third group had even less of a commitment. These were the 'preppies', who might be very enthusiastic, but nevertheless did not live the punk ideal as the other two groups did. Preppies were predominantly middle class (the other two were largely working class or lower middle class) and held down conventional jobs or were at school or college. This meant that they had to be able to switch on the punk image at will rather than by having it as a permanent feature of their appearance. Preppies were regarded by the inner two rings as inauthentic, and they were the frequent object of ridicule. However, they were critical to the existence of the group as a whole since they acted as a bridge with conventional society, providing financial assistance and other forms of help. Lastly, the largest group, the outer ring, were not punks at all but spectators who were interested but essentially non-participant. In effect, they provided an audience whenever the group met in the bar.[13]

Talk about authenticity is not just restricted to youth cultures but is a much more general characteristic. For example, when rock bands start out, they tend to place great emphasis on innovation and originality which they contrast with merely commercial work. Their identity as 'proper' musicians is bound up with authenticity.[14] As with Becker's jazz musicians, this insistence on authenticity can easily be at the expense of earning a living. The two can also be, in an ironic twist, perfectly compatible. Thus one study[15] by Simon Frith and Howard Horne noted the importance of art schools to the development of rock music in Britain from the 1960s. During this period, art schools provided a supportive environment for people (largely men) who had been rebellious or non-conformist at school. The colleges provided space for performance, and student audiences were more tolerant than others and more receptive to musical innovation or novelties in performance. The art school background gave the innovatory edge, which, in turn, generated commercial success.

It is important to re-emphasize how subtle these strategies of belonging are. Of course, people do not decide together to use certain patterns of language or to promulgate particular attitudes as marks of belonging and identity. These are processes that run under the surface of everyday life and are part of the *culture* of a group. That culture is taken for granted and only rises to the surface when challenged or compared with that of another group.

In thinking about groups of which we might be members, in imagination or more concretely, we are in effect thinking about the *boundaries* of those groups. Inside the boundary are all those people who are more or less like us. Establishing a boundary is another way in which belonging is claimed and established. A variety of mechanisms are used to police such boundaries. The authenticity claims discussed above function in this way. When a punk is dismissive of those who are punks only at weekends, he is effectively drawing a boundary between those who live the alternative life and those who are only playing at it. Other social groups will use shame and gossip to police a boundary. Those whose behaviour is out of line will be subject to joking commentaries or, at worst, will be ostracized. A study of a Punjabi community in Southall, west London, for example, notes how gossip and rumour are used to control young people, particularly as far as relations between the sexes are concerned. Gossip consists in fragments of information about the private lives of individuals which circulate among a relatively small network of people. Gossip becomes rumour when these fragments are put together in a composite picture of someone, which then circulates among a much wider group of people. In the exchange of gossip norms of behaviour are stated and confirmed. Rumour, in turn, controls because no one wishes to lose respect in the community. Families will do a great deal to make sure that their daughters in particular are not the subject of such rumours.[16] The crossing of other boundaries may involve the breaking of powerful taboos which will bring public shame on those involved. For example, in the southern states of America, a liaison, let alone a marriage, between a white woman and a black man was regarded, and still is, as a major offence to local custom, resulting in shame and humiliation or worse. Boundaries can be powerful, in other words, because they define all within the boundary as pure and all outside as impure and dangerous.

Some social groups, and hence identities, separate themselves off drastically; the boundaries are relatively firm and well policed. The groups are *encapsulated* and support encapsulated identities. For other identities, the boundary is weaker, more permeable and less easy to define and control. Thus, a study of religious movements by Roy Wallis contrasts world-rejecting movements, on the one hand, with world-affirming and world-accommodating movements, on the other. The former have rigid and heavily policed boundaries. Converts are expected to renounce their past lives and emotional ties, including those of their family, and the outside world is seen as threatening. The submerging of personal identity is sometimes reflected in the similarity of appearance or dress or in the way that converts take new names. Conversion tends to be sudden, involving a sharp break with a convert's past life. The Moonies and Krishna Consciousness are examples. World-affirming (such as Transcendental Meditation) and world-accommodating movements (the Jesus People, for instance), on the other hand, have much more fluid and permeable boundaries. For the former, the emphasis is on release of individual powers through religious participation and, for the latter, it is on individual religious experience. There is not such a thorough separation from the world and participation is likely to be part-time. Conversion can be gradual and managed through a network of friends and relatives.[17]

## Identity as difference

The argument of the previous section is that identity is formed through a sense of belonging to a collectivity of people who are similar. But similarity only makes sense together with difference. The boundary around the collectivity to which I belong is also a boundary that keeps others out. It is also fairly obvious that, while attitudes to those within the boundary are usually positive, a much more negative tone is generally adopted to those outside. These stereotypes may at one time have been based on the behaviour of one or two individuals but come to be ascribed to whole communities or groups, and are often very resistant to change or contrary evidence. The expression of such negative attitudes is a routine aspect of everyday life. Thus, people will have stereotypical views of the inhabitants of the local authority estate nearby, or, if Lancastrian, of Yorkshiremen. However, the question of identity as difference presents itself particularly acutely – and often violently – in such issues as ethnicity, religion and nationalism.

In Northern Ireland there are two distinct communities, one Protestant and one Catholic. Each very much has the marks of belonging that I have discussed. For example, a Protestant house will be filled with towels decorated with Union Jacks, photographs of the queen, or plaques with quotations from the Bible. Similarly, a Catholic house will have a picture of President Kennedy, or an image of a saint. The clothes that people wear, the tunes that are whistled, and references to historical events all reinforce belonging. They also reinforce difference and are accompanied by a systematic view of the other community as almost universally comprised of people who wish to inflict harm. For example,

Protestants will complain that Catholics do not want to work, are spongers and are priest-ridden. Catholics, on the other hand, will regard Protestants as bigots who discriminate against Catholics. Intriguingly, these stereotypical attitudes, Catholic or Protestant, tend to be expressed in private or in the company of members of the same religious community, a tendency reinforced by the lack of contact between the two communities. More public attitudes will be more restrained and will acknowledge, perhaps, that there are differences within the opposing community.[18]

A rather less extreme example of the way that difference supports identity is provided by a study of the way in which different communities within a housing estate saw each other.[19] So, people living in the south of the estate in houses that were relatively small and cheap saw themselves as plain folk, down-to-earth and economical with money. They saw those living in the larger and more expensive houses in the north of the estate as stuck up, interested only in what was new, extravagant and phoney. In turn, the northerners thought of themselves as refined and cultured and dedicated to family values. They saw the southerners, by contrast, as uncouth, with a tendency to allow their houses to go to rack and ruin and their children to run amuck.

It is fashionable to talk about globalization, a process which is supposed to be destroying the sense that we all belong to distinct nations with radically different cultures, traditions and histories.[20] In fact, nationalism is remarkably resistant to such homogenizing tendencies. This is demonstrated in the apparently trivial as well as the demonstrably serious. For example, although American and, to a lesser extent, British popular music appears to dominate the world, actually indigenous, national music continues to flourish.[21] At the other extreme, the recent violent history of Yugoslavia, as it broke up into a set of small nation-states, demonstrates the continuing power of nationalism, especially when supported by parallel ethnic and religious difference.

Although an acute sense of national difference accompanies violent conflict in human history, nationalism is better seen as a routine, background occurrence.[22] It is manifested in a number of ways – flag-waving at sporting events, the defence of national currencies, and civic rituals such as coronations, the opening of parliament or national days. It even creeps into the very language used every day to describe ourselves. For example, newspapers tend to be saturated with nationalist references. Thus, there is a persistent use of the words 'our' or 'we'. The assumption made is that the newspaper is addressing a nation with a strong sense of collective identity which can be contrasted with others. Again, there tend to be a large number of stories which mention 'Britain' or 'British'. Many countries of the world manifest regional differences which are very similar to expressions of nationalism and which can have real effects in turning regions into nations. For example, Scotland has long had a claim to be a separate nation, despite not being differentiated from the rest of the United Kingdom by major differences in language or religion. Opinion surveys regularly show that a substantial proportion of the Scottish population describe themselves as Scottish rather than British. Such an opinion is supported by attitudes of community with fellow Scots and of difference from the English. As a respondent in one study said:

> When I do go abroad I can introduce myself as Scottish and people will know what that means and know what kind of person they expect me to be, but I think I couldn't say the same if I was to go over and introduce myself as British, I couldn't imagine, think what that means and people obviously normally assume that you are English and speak English and are referred to as English.[23]

The argument so far, then, is that there are mechanisms for keeping some people inside boundaries and for keeping other people out. It follows that the process of crossing boundaries is of considerable interest. I have, in effect, already mentioned this process. Becker's account of being a marihuana user, for example, shows that the process of crossing the boundary from non-user to user is a process of social learning. But many boundaries are not so easily negotiated and identities not so easily changed. Sometimes it is positively dangerous. If a Protestant marries a Catholic in Northern Ireland, for example, they are likely to be cast out from both communities. Where there is an acceptance that boundaries will be crossed, the passage can be surrounded by ritual and symbolism. In many societies, for instance, coming of age, moving from a child to an adult, is signalled by a ceremony in which others effectively witness a change in identity.

## Identity and social change

This chapter has been about the *social* construction of identity. If my arguments are correct, it follows that identity is malleable – it changes over time as individuals move through different social circumstances. While this is true of any society, it may be the case that identities are more fluid in some societies than others. There are two steps in such an argument. First, the modern world is changing constantly and is becoming more diverse. Previously fixed points in everyday life are becoming unstable. Second, modern societies encourage, and even demand, that people actively construct their identities.

It is a commonplace that rapid change is the mark of contemporary society. For instance, in modern Britain, people move house, lose and gain jobs, get married and divorced, and travel more extensively than they did even fifty years ago. At the same time, society is more fragmented and diverse. For example, population movements have brought people of all sorts of cultures, ethnicities and religions to Britain. It is no longer the case that the typical family consists of a man and a woman with two children, as is depicted in so many insurance advertisements or in my account of the Wenhaston family at the beginning of this book. There is instead a great variety of family and household forms, ranging from single people and single parents to marriages between gay partners. The combination of change and diversity produces a less stable world in which traditional affiliations no longer have the meaning that they had. Critically, then, the relatively stable social groups, which in the past encouraged a sense of belonging and constructed identity, are being undermined. The outcome is that people's trajectories through life are much less predictable and much more individualized.

This point can be illustrated by looking at the way in which age is a less good predictor of social situation than it was. For example, those in their forties or early fifties have become a more diverse group than their parents had been at the same age. Some will have taken early retirement, some will be retraining, some will be progressing through careers, some will be temporarily unemployed. Domestic situations will be similarly various. Some people will have been married to the same partner since their early twenties, some will have remained single, some will be childless, some will be gay or lesbian. Ken Roberts applies the same argument to young people.[24] There is no longer a 'normal' situation for a person aged between sixteen and thirty. This change stems from a number of factors. Youth has become a stage in life that is more varied in length. In many respects it has become extended as more young people stay in education and marry and have children late. But at the same time there are significant numbers who do not continue in education beyond sixteen and will have children at that age or not much later. Second, young people's biographies have become *individualized*. The greater diversity of educational, occupational and family experience means that, in any one locality, there is no longer a collective experience. Third, there is greater uncertainty about the future that arises out of the pace of change which means that young people are being forced to take more risks. Particular careers which have traditionally been safe, banking for example, are so no longer. Personal relationships are not so likely to be permanent. These changes in the social situation of young people have had an impact on youth cultures. The age-range of those involved is greater; gender and social class differences are less marked; there is greater fragmentation of cultures as taste in clothes, music, and personal appearance becomes more and more differentiated.

In a changing and diverse world of this kind, identity is achieved by the activities of individuals rather than ascribed – given by circumstances. Individuals have to make their identity rather more since they cannot rely on a stable and coherent sense of belonging. This point is put theoretically by Tony Giddens.[25] He argues that, in modern society, individuals are reflexive, in that they constantly examine their own practices and alter them as a result. In doing so, people understand themselves, construct their self-identity, by working and reworking their interpretation of their own biography in the form of a narrative or story. The result is a 'trajectory of the self', a path of development from the past to an anticipated future, but the narratives that are constructed are inherently fragile and have to be worked at continuously.

In the film *About a Boy*, based on Nick Hornby's book of the same title, the central character appears to construct his identity in this way. He is in his late thirties, seems never to have had a stable relationship, lives alone on a private income derived from the success of a popular song written by his father, and is not located in a social group, or set of overlapping social groups, which gives him a sense of belonging and identity. His identity is constructed out of his leisure pursuits; in fact his life is defined by leisure, since he does not work. He is particular about his flat and its style and furnishings, and about his car, and his taste in music is especially important, as are his clothes. Style, attitudes, taste give him a sense of who he is. And they do so by conveying a sense of belonging because he can imagine others like him. But, at the end of the film, he makes a categorical choice which defines him. Through his relationship with a young boy, whom others believe wrongly to be his son, he becomes involved with a group of friends of very different ages and backgrounds. Indeed, they become almost a pseudo-family in that the last scene shows them all having Christmas dinner in his flat. Here, then, is a social group which gives belonging and identity but which is chosen, not given by background, work or locality.

This argument about the peculiarities of modern identity is seductive and plausible. However, it is possible to get carried away by it, and I need to sound two points of warning. First, one should not exaggerate the scope of the change. Although many sociologists do argue that a chosen lifestyle is critical for the formation of identity, actually group memberships, even traditional ones, remain important. Much of the evidence shows that family background, educational attainment, and occupation remain important in the determination of fundamental attitudes to life that are part of identity. I return to these points in future chapters. Second, because individuals are active in identity construction does not mean that identity is no longer socially negotiated. Indeed, the process of social construction is more obvious than ever, and the basic arguments outlined in this chapter still hold. Even if it were true that style and taste were fundamentally determining of identity, it would still be the case that they give a sense of belonging and are negotiated with others.

Nonetheless, something *is* different about modern life and one can interpret this change in the social construction of identity in different ways. On the one hand, it can be seen as a positive development. If individuals are freed from traditional social locations of class, ethnicity, community, sexuality – even gender – they are correspondingly free to invent themselves. A more fragmented society gives greater choice and possibility for personal development. On the other hand, it can be argued that the modern identity is rootless and that modern men and women, cast out from the stable social positions of the past, are insecure and anxious. These are not contradictory ideas, however. As I shall argue in subsequent chapters, the truth is really a combination of the two. Modern societies do indeed give greater opportunities, but, at the same time, they also create insecurity and anxiety.

# Who do we love?

Love: that self-love à deux
Madame de Staël

## Intimacy and romance

In the film *When Harry Met Sally* the two central characters, Harry and Sally, first meet each other as young students at university. After an initial period of mutual dislike, clearly actually based on mutual attraction, they become friends. After university they drift apart but see each other occasionally by accident, and each of them works through a series of lovers. Then, since they end up in the same city, they see more of each other and become close friends. Eventually, the inevitable happens and, realizing that their relationship is not 'just' friendship, they become lovers.

What is the nature of the relationship between the two? The film focuses intensively on the two central characters and especially on what they *say* to each other. Indeed, the film is primarily made up of conversation; very little else happens. In these conversations, they are aiming to declare themselves and their innermost feelings, to analyse their characters and personalities, to know each other really well, whether they are friends or lovers. Authenticity and truth are highly valued; warmth and trust are priorities. Descriptions of how one *feels* are staples of everyday life, and the narrative of the film is constructed to display feeling, not action. The view of personal relationships that is embodied in the film could be described as *intimacy*. And this is true, not just of the relationship between the two central characters, but also of the relationships of those two with their friends.

In contemporary societies, intimacy is positively valued. The contrast is with relationships that are cold, distant, formal, polite, superficial or inauthentic. As an ideal of human conduct, intimacy is beginning to seep out of very personal relationships into more public arenas. Consider the way that politicians address their electorates. Politicians' speeches, indeed, are not really addresses. They are, rather, modelled as conversations between friends and equals, in which the politician tries to create a sense of a warm relationship with the members of the audience as individuals. For example, all current British politicians use conversational turns of phrase such as 'You know . . .' or 'Look . . .'. Public comment on political leadership is more about the personality of the politician than it is about his achievement. Again, television in many ways is not a public medium of communication. It is rather more domestic, private and conversational. Frequently, therefore, presenters appear to be engaging in a private interchange with each and every viewer, looking directly into the camera.

The way in which politicians or television presenters speak to us seems entirely natural, and it is tempting to think that the way that people see their personal relationships – what they are trying to get out of them – is a fact of human nature and will not vary much from society to society. Intimacy, however, is very much a modern attitude, and a contrast may be made with the view of personal relationships prevailing in the eighteenth and early nineteenth centuries.[1] Relationships then were rather more etiquette-governed, formal and well mannered. An example may help to make this clearer. In Jane Austen's novels, personal relationships are formal and regulated. Elizabeth's parents in *Pride and Prejudice* call each other Mr and Mrs Bennett, as would any eighteenth- or early nineteenth-century married couple. In *Sense and Sensibility*, immoderate declarations of feeling or claims to intimacy, especially when made in public, are treated as stepping outside the bounds of decorum and as potentially dangerous and self-harming. This does not mean to say that personal relationships of this formal kind are not pleasurable or loving. But the pleasure does not derive from the pursuit of intimacy; that is not the *point* of personal relationships. Pleasure does flow from treating relationships as a *performance* which was highly governed by convention. Life was theatre. For example, conversation in the eighteenth century was treated as an art form.[2] Treatises on the art appeared which recommended sets of rules, a common one being the avoidance of speaking of oneself – an unlikely rule for modern, intimate talk. The 'art of conversation', on the other hand, is a rarely used phrase in the twenty-first century. Conversation is rather a means to an end, a way of demonstrating or accomplishing intimacy; it is not valued for its own sake. This does, incidentally, give a different quality to relationships in public and with strangers. A more controlled and conventional attitude makes relationships with strangers possible, and potentially pleasurable, because a set of rules is available to all and everybody knows what to expect. In modern society, because intimacy is the ideal model of relationships and because such intimacy requires a pre-established trust, relationships with strangers, particularly in public, tend to be potentially threatening. Erving Goffman points to a way that people in contemporary public settings manage relationships with strangers. They manifest what he calls 'civil inattention'. This involves a recognition that a stranger is there but otherwise no attention is paid. Civil inattention thus avoids the two extremes of staring at the stranger, on the one hand, or looking through them, on the other, both of which would be breaches of civility.

It is risky to exaggerate the difference between personal relationships as intimate, on the one hand, and as artful and controlled, on the other. In the contemporary world, excess of passion is still not approved of and truth-telling is moderated by appreciation of its possible consequences. Similarly, in the eighteenth and nineteenth centuries, at least for the middle and upper classes, there was really a tension between a romantic view of personal relationships and a controlled and artful one. Rather what we have is a spectrum from the intimate, at one end, to the regulated, at the other, and the ideal and the practice of contemporary society is closer to the intimate end. And we should note that intimacy requires conditions that may be peculiarly modern. First, it depends on equality between the partners. Innermost secrets are not to be disclosed by a subordinate person to one who dominates them, and those who hold power or authority over others will be undermined by revealing too much of themselves. For example, couples in a marriage or cohabitation may find it more difficult to be intimate in this sense if there is substantial economic inequality between them. That implies that intimacy requires the partners to the relationship to be relatively independent of one another. Intimacy, in other words, does not involve the submerging of one person into another. At the same time, intimacy is a demanding relationship. Its rewards may be great but so are its risks. Partners ask a great deal of each other, and satisfaction in the relationship depends on a good deal of trust between them. On the one hand, the relationship demands commitment to give the trust so necessary to sustain intimacy. On the other hand, because the relationship is voluntary, it can always be broken, a situation which can give a sense of unpredictability and impermanence. Such relationships are, therefore, on a knife-edge; they are inherently vulnerable and insecure and hence more likely to break up.[3]

Of course, one way in which the ideal of intimacy is thought to be realized is in romantic love. Modern ideas of romantic love, as they are deployed in books, films and songs, imply a baring of souls, a sharing of innermost secrets. The typical plot of tales of romantic love consists in a quest, involving setbacks and triumphs, in which a man and a woman succumb to an overmastering love for each other, which may be permanent but which also may be tragic in its conclusion.

The ideals of romantic love provide a way of thinking about relationships. How, then, are these ideals acted out, if at all? A familiar argument is that a woman is impelled by a belief in romance to form a relationship with a man. She is then disappointed by the man's failure to manifest emotional intimacy. Much of the research bears this out. Many women interviewed in one study, for example, felt deserted after the initial – and short-lived – burst of romance. Our society offers images of passionate romantic love but no ideas about how to live happily ever after. Here, for example, is one woman talking in an interview:

> We went through the romantic bit to start with . . . but he loved his *work* and that was the problem . . . he still loved me in the sense of, you know, the *picture* was right . . . a successful businessman with a wife who could entertain and nice little children, always lots of presents, lots of money spent on 'em because the emotional wasn't spent on 'em, so he thought as long as he was spending money, everything must be all right . . .[4]

At the best, some women in this study felt that their relationship had settled into a steady companionship, a friendship, which, however, still lacked a serious emotional commitment in which their needs were met. Instead they put their energies into children, work or friends. The result is that very large numbers of women profess dissatisfaction with their marriages. One American survey found that 98 per cent of women wanted fundamental changes in their marriage and 96 per cent felt that they were giving more emotional support to their partners than they were receiving.[5]

Research into men's attitudes and behaviour appears to support the views that women express. One study that investigated the relationship between schooling, masculinity and sexuality[6] found that the public talk of male school students to each other was misogynistic, boasting of sexual conquests in which women were treated as the passive objects of male desires. This view of women was closely associated with a particular macho interpretation of masculinity and an apparent homophobia. However, when interviews were conducted in private, this uniform picture began to fragment and the young men looked less certain and confident in their views. Many of them commented on the paradoxical loneliness of being in their peer group. They found that they could not express their feelings to each other and they felt unloved and deprived. They were emotionally illiterate in not having the language or the opportunity to talk about their inner fears and feelings. Similarly, their private sexuality was also not quite so securely asserted. Some would concede that they had felt sexually attracted to other men, although that might not fundamentally alter their sexuality. More significantly, however, they were confused about expressing affection for their male friends, given that such an expression might be misinterpreted.

Much everyday and public discussion assumes too easily that there are sharp distinctions to be made, especially in the case of masculinity and sexuality. It is as if there is only one way of being a man or a woman. The research shows, however, that there is actually a multitude of masculinities and femininities formed by cross-cutting differences such as class, ethnicity, nationality, age and so on. To take but one example, so far I have presented the evidence and argument as if a wish for romantic love was restricted to women. In one study, however, a particular group of boys from professional or managerial backgrounds indicated the power that romantic images had over them in their relationships with girls. For example, here is one comment from a participant in the study on the initial stages in a relationship:

> Falling in love is a natural process, yeah, it clicks. It's not something you can achieve. It is something that falls into place. One day you wake up and think, 'Wow!'. You know, you can work at it but it can't be the same as real, natural love. It just comes naturally . . . It just happens . . . it comes from inside you definitely. It's just a magnetism.[7]

Furthermore, this romantic imagery is associated with attitudes that express an emotional intimacy that spills over into other relationships:

> I suppose going out with my girlfriend at the moment has like changed my outlook to friends. Instead of treating them like shit, you treat them rightly . . . I just used to expect them to listen to me, but whenever they had a problem I'd just go [affects an uninterested look], 'Yeah, yeah'.[8]

At the same time, not all *women* manifest an attachment to romance. One study shows the way that working-class women who grew up in Britain before the Second World War repudiated romance as silly and possibly destructive.[9] They aspired instead to material comfort and secure domesticity, and romantic love could threaten these outcomes by introducing the possibility of irrational choices.

Of course, traditionally, romantic love between heterosexual couples is supposed to lead to marriage. Actually, the way in which people reflect on marriage has only elements of romance. According to one study of the attitudes of newly-wed couples,[10] there is a continual interaction between images of what marriage should be like, what it could be like, and what it probably will be like. An important constituent of expectations of marriage is that it perpetuates a tradition – a tradition of family formation, however that tradition is interpreted by the people concerned. You come from a family, so you need to create one in your turn. In addition, for the respondents in this study, another reason for the continuing attractiveness of marriage is that it permits a validation of adulthood. Marriage is not the only way of becoming adult but, at a stroke, it permits the setting up of an independent life and a separation from parents and the parental home. At the start of their married lives, newly-weds are expected to have romantic images of marriage, of the 'happily-ever-after' variety. In fact, in this study, very few romantic images of this kind are revealed. The partners do have ideals of marriage. In particular, the women tend to have a companionate model of marriage, one based on caring and sharing. Such a view is certainly consistent with the ideal of intimacy in personal relationships. It is not, however, especially romantic. Hardly surprisingly, marriage is the everyday reality; romance is the extraordinary event or feeling.

## Intimacy and partnership

As an institution, marriage is changing. The traditional image of marriage as a culmination of a romantic attachment, lasting for the lifetime of the partners and involving two or three children, no longer matches reality, as frequent articles in newspapers attest. A number of factors have produced this change. First, many people prefer not to engage in marriage to start with. In the mid-1960s, some 5 per cent of women had lived with their husband-to-be before marriage. Thirty years later, the figure is 70 per cent. Some commentators think that this change is an indication that marriage as an institution is in permanent decline.[11] A preference for cohabitation may be explained by the changing roles of men and women. Traditional marriage is essentially patriarchal and is underpinned by the economic power of men. However, women are entering into long-term careers in increasing numbers and this gives them economic power. Cohabitation gives greater independence to both partners and is therefore better suited to a situation in which women have an improved bargaining position. At the same time as the economic balance in marriage is changing, so also is the domestic balance as men – slowly – take on more household tasks.

In the recent past, marriage may have been a route to adulthood, and hence people got married relatively young. With education and work giving alternative routes, especially to women, people are marrying later – and this is not entirely due to the prevalence of cohabitation before marriage. Late marriage is also associated with the rapid increase in the numbers of children born to couples who are not married. In the late 1990s, 40 per cent of births were outside marriage, more than twice the proportion in the mid-1970s.

Third, marriages – and cohabitations – are increasingly unstable. On present trends, it is likely that almost half of the marriages contracted in the United Kingdom this year will end in divorce. Furthermore, more recent marriages tend to last less long before divorce ends them, and the rate of divorce has increased fastest in younger age-groups.[12] These trends indicate that the rate of divorce may rise still further and that it is younger marriages that will be most affected.

Fourth, if the presence of children helps to define the traditional marriage, their absence betokens social change. Roughly one in five women born in 1975 remains childless, a higher proportion than in the recent past. This increase is unlikely to be due only to work commitments. According to one recent study, childless couples are not especially work-orientated. They do, however, prize their egalitarian partnership, which might be undermined by children, and regard parenthood as demanding and constraining of their freedom and individuality.[13]

Lastly, a larger proportion of the population is single and living alone. In 1961, 11 per cent of households contained one person. By 1981 this had risen to 22 per cent. By 1998 it was 29 per cent. By 2020, about one-third of households are forecast to be made up of one person.[14] Some of this growth is due to the ageing of the population; with a greater proportion of elderly people, there is a corresponding increase in the numbers of widows and widowers. However, the most significant growth is among those under retirement age. Again, the divorced are likely to be left alone following the departure of their partners. For others, living alone may be a transition phenomenon. For example, the divorced may remarry, and the majority do. Or, young people may live alone after leaving home or university and before moving in with a partner. Or, for yet other people, living alone may be a positive lifestyle choice. It is this last category that is most significant, especially for those under forty. In 1971, only 3 per cent of the twenty-five to twenty-nine age-group was living alone; in 1991 this had risen to 11 per cent, with a disproportionate increase among women. It is important to realize that the choice to live alone can be accompanied by relationships of intimacy, a point to which I return at the end of this chapter.

These changes do transform the traditional model of marriage. Paradoxically, though, people show a remarkable degree of unrealistic affection for the institution. Opinion surveys show that the great majority of people expect to get married, stay married to the same partner and have children. In the eighteenth century, Dr Johnson noted that second marriages were the triumph of hope over experience. In the twenty-first, it looks as if that is true of first marriages as well. However, the crucial question is: does the apparent transformation of the institution of marriage undermine the notions of intimacy or romantic love? Paradoxically it probably reinforces them. None of these changes constitute a rejection of a personal relationship based on intimacy. For example, divorce is only a repudiation of a particular partner, not a dismissal of the idea of partnership. Indeed, most divorced people seek out another partner. Furthermore, the gradually increasing equality and independence within partnerships of all kinds, which is one of the reasons for changes within the traditional marriage, actually fosters intimacy.

## Private love

Intimacy is a *private* relationship. One consequence of this is that, as there is greater stress on intimacy as the proper way in which to define personal relationships, so the circle of those we love has become more private. One way in which to describe this process is through the idea of family privatism, the idea that social life is increasingly centred on the conjugal family and the home.

I have already argued that the relationship between partners – an index of family privatism – will be increasingly characterized by intimacy. The implication is that the relationship – what one could call the conjugal tie – becomes more significant in the lives of the partners and carries a greater emotional weight. What might that mean in practice? A conclusion of earlier studies of the family in the 1950s and 1960s in Britain was that social ties outside the family, with wider family and friends, were becoming attenuated as married couples concentrated on their relationship with each other, their children and their homes.[15] The same studies also argued that this increasing domesticity was accompanied by a growing equality between husband and wife within the marriage. A symmetrical family was emerging in which the roles of husband and wife are less sharply differentiated.

This conclusion has now become a staple of public comment. Later research has been able to contribute more precise evidence. For example, recent studies by Gershuny seek to measure changes in the domestic division of labour – the balance between husband and wife in the carrying out of domestic tasks – by reanalysing a set of studies, done at different times, all of which look at the use of *time* in the household.[16] He investigates what he calls the dual burden hypothesis, which states that, even as wives take on full-time jobs, they continue to carry the burden of domestic work. Gershuny concludes that this hypothesis is only partially correct. The critical point is that, over the period 1974 to 1987, the proportion of domestic work carried out by husbands rose in a context of increased paid work by wives. It could be argued that the growth in men's work is actually not in the core tasks of cleaning and cooking but rather is concentrated in odd jobs, repairs and decorating. Again, Gershuny's data do not bear this out. Over the period 1974 to 1987, husbands of full-time employed wives doubled the amount of time they spent in cooking and cleaning.

Gershuny concludes that, although women still carry out the principal burden of domestic work, there is a lagged adaptation to their increasing paid work as men take on more household tasks. And it is worth stressing that there may well be an increasing tendency to greater equality between men and women, but that does not mean that there is absolute equality. Studies of such diverse areas of domestic life as decision-making,[17] money management,[18] choices about food,[19] and even the use of the television remote control,[20] show that men continue to dominate. Men's adaptation to women's entry into paid employment, in other words, is slow and is uneven across different social groups. For example, unemployed men tend not to take on domestic tasks even when their partners are employed.

Family privatism also means that parents concentrate more on children than in previous periods, or do so in a different way. Historians have long argued that European societies have had different conceptions of childhood at different points in their histories.[21] There is not, in other words, a single 'natural' way of treating children. To modern sensibilities, cruelty to children is an abomination. The fact is, though, that this sense is a social construction. What seems cruel to one society – very young children working in factories, for instance – may seem perfectly normal to another, as the debates that took place in the nineteenth century in Britain indicate only too well. The modern view of childhood, then, is that it is a relatively long and distinct phase in human development with its own peculiar characteristics. Children are not simply little adults in the making. They require special treatment involving special agencies like schools, nurseries and social workers. Their correct treatment is the subject of a large number of books and magazines. The conduct of adults towards them is regulated by a system of law. And everybody worries about them.

Historians debate when this modern view of childhood appeared. Some argue that it is in the twelfth century, while others favour a much later date, the eighteenth or early nineteenth century. In some ways, this search for the date of the discovery of modern childhood is misleading, since it seems to imply that all of history is leading up to the present set of conventions of how to treat children. It is better to see different epochs as having different views of how long childhood lasts, how children differ from adults and how significant these differences are.

There can be little doubt, however, that the modern view of childhood admits children to the circle of loved ones within the private family. Photographs of children will be central to the family album, while reminiscences and letters of previous centuries may not have mentioned children at all. Families are smaller and the child becomes the focus of attention from parents. This is the age of the anxious parent. If one goes into any large newsagent one will be greeted by any number of magazines on parenting, all of which suggest the extreme importance of getting it right. The implication is that the health, safety, and psychological, social and intellectual development of the child are paramount, but these things do not happen by themselves. The parents make them happen, and if things go wrong it is their fault. Some of these anxieties come out in the readers' letters in the magazines in that they betray a lack of confidence in things happening by themselves and a consequent close focusing on the child.

The argument so far, then, is that love is becoming increasingly private and located in the domestic sphere. At any one time, of course, there are substantial sections of the population which are not in this kind of domestic setting. Young people and older people living alone or childless couples are obvious examples. It is quite clear that people like this do form intense relationships with those that they do not live with. However, the critical point, I think, is that most people will spend much of their lives in a domestic relationship with a partner and involved with children. Such a tendency is reinforced by ideals of domestic life and a concentration on the home. Of course the idea of home is not new. For two centuries, perhaps, it has been a refuge, it has been the physical place of the family and household, the place we leave in the morning and return to at night and a place of familiar and comforting routine. It is frequently a sentimental image. Take this passage from *The Wind in the Willows*, when Mole is on a dangerous and difficult journey which takes him away from his beloved home and then suddenly he is reminded of it.

> Shabby indeed, and poorly furnished, and yet his, the home he had made for himself, the home he had been so happy to get back to after his day's work . . . how much it all meant to him, and the special value of some such anchorage in one's existence.[22]

It is arguable, however, that this ideal of home has been further emphasized in the second half of the twentieth century. Homes have increasingly become places of privacy, security and creativity.[23] They are private in the sense that there is a clear understanding that there are restrictions on entry. They are secure because the home gives those who live there a sense of control. They provide scope for creativity because the inhabitants take pleasure in making their home as attractive as possible. Thus, there has been an increasing tendency for people to own their homes, more pronounced in Britain than in other European countries. In 1996, for example, about 70 per cent of Britons owned their own homes compared with 55 per cent in France and 40 per cent in Germany. There is more interest in domestic style and furnishing represented in an apparently daily deluge of television programmes on buying and selling houses, creating gardens and perfecting interior decoration. Many owner-occupiers spend a great deal of time working on their houses. Some owners do this because they cannot afford to buy the professional services. But, as one study found, the majority of house owners derive great satisfaction from doing it themselves. As one of the respondents in this study found:

> I stood and looked at the kitchen ceiling for a quarter of an hour last night after I'd finished it. I know it's silly but it's the satisfaction you get. And I wouldn't feel like that if I didn't own the place.[24]

Houses are filled with consumer durables, many of which provide for home-based leisure. About 70 per cent of leisure time is spent in the home, mostly watching the television. In fact, almost as much time is spent watching television as all other domestic leisure pursuits put together. As one commentator put it, fifty years ago we worked and slept; now we work and sleep – and watch television. In the early years of the twenty-first century, for example, the average person will spend almost 25 hours per week in front of the set. People talk extensively about television programmes they have seen and have not seen, and they rely on them for news and information. There is a sense in which television is central to people's lives, and this is reflected in the nature of television itself, for it is a profoundly *domestic* medium. Although it is tempting to see television as a sort of film, it is actually nothing of the kind. First, television is so much part of everyday life that we take it entirely for granted. It forms part of the household routine and helps, in many households, to mark out the passage of time. So much of television output is really illustrated talk. Second, many programmes – situation comedy, soap opera, gardening, home decoration, for example – are very much concerned with the family, home and domestic life. Third, the style of television is often that of a conversation with the viewer. Announcers, weathermen and women, newsreaders, talk-show hosts and many others face the camera directly and are therefore giving the illusion of having an intimate, direct, domestic conversation with the person watching. This sense of direct address is reinforced by the conversational language employed by television. Much television actually *is* conversation. Soap opera and situation comedy largely consist in conversation, often in private, domestic spaces. Other sorts of television are constructed as simulated conversations in which the participants pretend to be having the kind of exchange that viewers might have round their kitchen table.

I have been arguing that contemporary society encourages family privatism in which emotional energy, time and love are directed inwards to the immediate family and the home. It is wise, however, not to overstate the case. The idea of family privatism tends to be overgeneralized. There are obvious differences between different types of household – retired, single-person, with young children, with children living away – in the way that there is a focus on home and family. Furthermore, one should beware of assuming too readily that a concentration on family necessarily goes together with an interest in domesticity and leads to a neglect of other relationships outside the family, as we shall see in the next chapter.[25] Lastly, although more intense in the present day, partly because of women's involvement in the labour market, family privatism has a long history. There is nothing uniquely new about wanting to spend time at home with one's family. One study of nineteenth-century Bristol, for example, concluded that the view of the Victorian neighbourhood as a friendly, mutually supportive and sociable place is misleading.[26] Neighbourhoods were often experienced as hostile and gossip-ridden, while the home was the secure and private realm. Furthermore, even by the 1920s, husbands were normally home- and family-centred, developing close relationships with their children.

## Friendship

The implication of the previous discussion is that love is the pursuit of intimacy but is increasingly restricted to the private sphere and especially the family. What does this imply for friendship?

At first sight, it might seem that the intimate, private family is replacing friendship. Perhaps, if people are turning inward, they have less time and emotional energy for their friends. For example, when asked to whom people would turn for practical, financial or emotional help, the great majority put their family members first. The only exception, hardly surprisingly, is difficulty with partners. Further, there is some evidence that people are seeing their friends less than they used to.[27]

Nonetheless, survey research continues to show that people can define a network of close relationships which includes friends as well as family. And this network is established partly by those who are excluded from it. Thus, a study of the community relationships of the elderly showed that friends, who are emotionally close and likely to offer support, are distinguished from neighbours, who are friendly but not close.[28] And relationships with close friends will exhibit the characteristics of intimacy described earlier. Close friends are those who can be counted upon in times of trial and who will share personal concerns and anxieties.

However, people may mean different things by friendship, have very different friendship styles and have different aims in seeking friendship. Patterns of friendship in the modern world vary across countries, social classes and age-groups and between men and women. For example, it is almost a truism that men and women have different styles of friendship. Women are more ready to share their innermost thoughts and secrets with each other; they look for *intimacy* with their friends. They may also believe that they can have the same kind of relationship with their male partners and they tend to come away disappointed. This doubtless explains the survey results which show that women are much more discontented with marriage than are men. On the whole, the research confirms this stereotypical view of gender differences in friendship. In childhood, for instance, girls form small, intimate and cooperative groups or pairs, while boys typically are involved in larger, more competitive groups focused on a set of activities. To a great extent this kind of gender difference persists in adulthood. Self-revelation is more common for women, while friendship for men is more concentrated on doing things together.

Similarly, there are social class differences in patterns of friendship. Middle-class people tend to have more friends than working-class ones and the friendships are organized differently. Middle-class friendships will start in particular settings such as work or a sports club. But they are then transferred to other settings as the friends arrange to meet to go to the theatre or to each other's homes. The meaning of middle-class friendship is not given by the original place of meeting but by the individuality of the people concerned, who can now interact in *any* situation. The same is not true of working-class people, whose social contacts tend to be confined within particular settings. In this case, people met at work or in the pub will not be asked home.[29]

## The self

This chapter is about the objects of love. It would be incomplete without mentioning the possibility that we love ourselves to the neglect of relationships with others. This is, of course, a frequently voiced public fear, particularly a literary fear. E. M. Forster, for example, in a short story entitled 'The Machine Stops', describes a future world in which people live in individual cells underground sustained by a machine which does everything for them – giving food, medical attention and entertainment. For Forster, the critical thing is that people have stopped having any relationships with each other, and the only salvation is a destruction of the society of separate individuals and a rediscovery of the dependence on each other – which is what happens in the story.

An argument common in both public debate and sociological analysis is that, in contemporary society, there is a greater emphasis on the individual and his or her rights, privileges, personal development and autonomy. The intimate relationship between couples that we have been describing, therefore, is a relationship, not of two selves that have been fused together, but of two individuals who maintain their independence and separateness.

The proposition that modern societies place a greater weight on the individual's autonomy and self-development has been framed by Giddens in his idea of 'the reflexive project of the self'.[30] Tony Giddens argues that the contemporary world is fragmented. To take one example of this fragmentation, we argued earlier that there is a much greater variety of households in modern Britain – cohabiting and non-married couples, gay couples, divorced people remarried with reconstituted families, single people living alone because they are divorced, widowed or have chosen to do so, and so on. At the same time as it is fragmented, the world is rapidly changing and is no longer governed by tradition or custom. People cannot rely on old ways for guidance on how to behave in any particular new situation. For Giddens, the result of these forces of fragmentation and de-traditionalization is the dominance of what he calls 'reflexivity'. In a fast-moving and fragmented world without traditional ways of behaving, everything that happens in modern society is the result of reflection; everything is examined anew and changed in the light of new information. For individuals, this means that they cannot take their identity for granted. When a person's identity cannot be defined by traditional means – occupation, locality, even gender, for example – it has to be worked at and continuously refashioned, and individuals come to be focused on this work of identity reconstruction. For Giddens, this is what a greater emphasis on the individual means; in contemporary societies, individuals become self-realizing, autonomous entities.

We can put some flesh on these theoretical bones by exploring what has become known as the postmaterialist hypothesis. This is the proposition that a very large proportion of the populations of Western countries have been raised in conditions of economic security and, therefore, while they may be concerned with physical and economic security, these have a lower priority than they had in the past. The result is a greater concentration on the quality of life, on the capacity that individuals have for self-realization and on aesthetic and non-material goals.

The postmaterialist hypothesis has been tested in a variety of studies. In one of these, respondents were asked a battery of questions designed to elicit values and attitudes ranging from a wish to move towards a society in which ideas count more than money to a desire to fight rising prices.[31] Inglehart detects a clear tendency for these values to be grouped. That is, if a respondent is postmaterialist on one issue, emphasizing individual quality of life rather than economic or physical security, it is likely that he or she will be postmaterialist on all. Postmaterialist responses are more common among younger age-groups. This is not because people become more materialistic as they grow older or because, as people move through the life cycle and acquire responsibilities, they become more interested in money. Rather it reflects a real generational change. Later generations are, and stay, more postmaterialistic than their predecessors. In addition, within any age-group, it is those raised in relatively prosperous families that are most likely to emphasize postmaterialist values. In turn, the move to postmaterialist values forms part of a more general cultural shift affecting Western societies. As Giddens noted, traditional religious and cultural norms, which at one time provided a form of stability and security, are in retreat.

This argument about a turn to the self seems to sit paradoxically with the earlier argument about intimacy as the basis for personal relationships. The two are, however, not inconsistent. Earlier on in this chapter, I noted that an increasing number of people were *choosing* to live alone. A recent study shows their reasons for doing so.[32] The interviews on which the study is based emphasize the importance of independence and freedom – to furnish their flats as they like, to eat when they want, and to see whom they want. They apparently exemplify the turn to the self. As one interviewee said: 'I think that it's important to kind of be an individual, I think there are too many people who are dependent upon other people.' It would be a great mistake, however, to see these people as in any way lonely. Quite the contrary: many of them have active social lives. Indeed, some of the living aloners were married, returning home at weekends, and others had long-distance relationships with partners. The turn to the self embodied in living alone is, in other words, not incompatible with pursuing intimate relationships. In fact, in stressing equality and independence, it may make that more possible.

In this chapter, I have argued that love between human beings is seen as intimacy. This is a particular kind of love that involves self-revelation. In this sense, the contemporary societies of the West have a distinctive way of loving that is different from that prevailing in other societies and from earlier periods of Western society. There is not, in other words, a single *natural* way of loving, whatever commonsense may tell us. Although friendship is highly valued in our society, intimacy, the circle of loved ones, is confined largely to private settings, chiefly the family. In the next chapter, I look at how we all relate to those who are less close.

# Who do we talk to?

For what do we live, but to make sport for our neighbours, and to laugh at them in our turn?

Jane Austen

In the last chapter I recounted the bare bones of a short story by E. M. Forster. Now, although it is easy to dismiss Forster's story as a dystopia written in the 1920s, as a grim warning perhaps but not an accurate description of modern society, nonetheless it does have resonances with some of my arguments so far. It is notable that the Wenhastons' daily life, described at the beginning of this book, is lived between work and education on the one hand and home on the other. At least as far as the adults are concerned, there is little in between and, though they may think about going out and talking to somebody else, they actually stay in and watch the television. In the last chapter I introduced the idea of family privatism, which could be used to describe the Wenhastons' daily life. The implication of that idea is that people have little time, energy, or emotional commitment to talk to (let alone love) others who are not work associates or immediate family members. There appears to be a shrinking down of people's social world.

It is possible to have a positive or a negative view of this privatism, and both views tend to be represented in public discussion. On the positive side, it has been argued that a concentration on family is natural to humanity. Families are the fundamental building blocks of society. They constitute a refuge from life's storms while producing and rearing the next generation. As long as the family unit is safe, it may be argued, it does not matter too much about contact with others. At the same time, the family is seen as a protector against oppression of the individual. Obligations to wider family, the pressures of an intrusive local community, and an overcontrolling state can all curtail the freedom of the individual, who can, nevertheless, be protected by the immediate family.

The pessimists, on the other hand, are worried about the apparent selfishness of a greater family privatism and of an increased emphasis on the rights and privileges of the individual. A shrinking of loyalties and commitments into a smaller unit implies that the ties of obligation to others will atrophy. A healthy society depends on active participation in voluntary organizations, on involvement in community projects, and in helping out friends and members of the wider family. Any decay in these ties outside the immediate family will have serious consequences, which will, in turn, affect the family. For example, there has been a public debate for some time about the care of the elderly. It is felt that families have forgotten their duty to care for older family members. As a result, the elderly are either left to fend for themselves or are consigned to the tender mercies of the state. Indeed, a healthy set of relationships outside the family will protect the individual from the excesses of family life. The pessimists will point to the tendency for families to become emotional hothouses which can seriously damage individuals. Violence towards children is only one of the most extreme examples of such damage.

Historically, sociologists have tended to side with the pessimists. Emile Durkheim, for instance, a French nineteenth-century sociologist, was fascinated by the question of social order – how is it that societies do not fly apart?[1] For him, a crucial part of an answer to this question was the network of social relationships between the individual and family, on the one hand, and the big institutions of the state and work, on the other. The more integrated individuals and families were with each other, the better for social health. Thus, he explored the way in which social order breaks down, the better to understand the mechanisms that preserve it. In one study[2] he took the rate of suicide as an index of social breakdown. He found that the rate of suicide was higher in Protestant countries than in Catholic ones. He did not attribute this to differing doctrines regarding suicide since, in his view, both religions condemned it as a sin. Rather he found the explanation of the difference in the degree of social integration promoted by the two religions. Catholic families and individuals were far more integrated into their wider society, while Protestants made a virtue of individual self-reliance. For Durkheim, then, the point about religion is not simply that it is a collection of beliefs or practices of worship but that it develops and strengthens social bonds.

More recent sociologists have retained an interest in the power of religion to promote social cohesion. It is frequently argued, therefore, that this power declined a great deal in European societies in the twentieth century, although one can hardly say the same of all societies in the world. In the United Kingdom, for instance, in 1998 only 7.5 per cent of the population attended church weekly, compared with 10 per cent in 1989 and 12 per cent in 1979.[3] Other indications of participation show the same trend. Within the Anglican church, infant baptisms, confirmations, and the numbers of ministers and churches have all fallen dramatically since the Second World War. It is true that other non-Christian religions show more vigour. The membership of the Sikh, Muslim and Hindu faiths has grown considerably within the last thirty years, and evangelical and charismatic branches of the Christian tradition have also shown some growth.[4] However, all these groupings still represent a small proportion of the population of the United Kingdom.

This decline in what might be called institutional adherence does not necessarily mean, however, that people are not still *privately* religious. Indeed, there is some evidence that religion has become more of a question of private feeling than of public worship or even public morality. According to a survey of religious belief and attitudes, 69 per cent of the population believe in God, 55 per cent in a life after death, 45 per cent in religious miracles and 28 per cent in the devil; 43 per cent describe themselves as religious, 28 per cent have had an intense religious experience and 27 per cent pray at least once a week.[5] These data hardly indicate a totally secular nation – even if one might argue that many of these beliefs owe as much to superstition as to religion. But the crucial point is that the *privatization* of religious belief and practice must surely diminish the capacity of religion to act as a kind of social cement. Religion will have the integrative functions that Durkheim ascribed to it, precisely because it is to do with a community of believers who see and interact with each other often and do not confine their religion to the private sphere.

The pessimists would therefore find, in the history of religion in the United Kingdom in the twentieth century, some confirmation of their argument. That intermediate network of social relationships, the protective layer between the family which can be a troublesome emotional hothouse, on the one hand, and, on the other, the large organizations of the state or of work, within which the individual can feel lost and oppressed, is apparently being attenuated. However, religious communities are not the only means by which families and individuals look outwards. On the contrary, the network is delicate but many-stranded. Outside their immediate families, therefore, people have networks of relationships with their friends, their wider family of grandparents, aunts, uncles and cousins, the neighbourhood and community, and the whole host of voluntary and spare-time organizations to which people give their time. In fact, it is probably best to see the whole network of relationships outside the home as overlapping sub-networks. After all, neighbours may simply be people who live nearby, but they may also be family; friends may be neighbours but they may also be involved in the same voluntary organizations. One should also not forget that, for most people, work is not just a means of earning money. It is also a source of social contact – and supportive social contact at that.

One may refer to the totality of relationships of this kind as an individual's social capital. The comparison with other forms of capital is deliberate. Just as an individual may use financial capital, so also may he or she use social capital. The networks of relationships may sometimes be of direct benefit. For example, most people pay particular attention to reciprocity when they ask others to social events. If I have someone round for a drink, I will expect to be asked in return. More commonly and subtly, the reciprocity is not attached to particular individuals but is more generalized. That is, in much of my social activity, I don't necessarily expect a tit-for-tat response. In working for a voluntary organization, for instance, I will not be thinking directly of any benefit to myself. Nonetheless, there is a general sense of give and take which is unconscious and taken for granted. In carrying out voluntary work, I expect that many others will be doing the same. The stock of human relationships that constitute social capital acts as a buffer, offering practical and emotional support. We should also note that, just as people will have different amounts of financial capital, so also can they have different quantities of social capital; some people have a less dense network of friends, neighbours and wider family than others. To the extent that social capital conveys benefit, then, it may well add to the inequalities in society.

So, are the pessimists right? Is the total stock of social capital in society in decline? Is the circle of those we talk to narrowing? To answer these questions I turn to a more detailed examination of different circles of relationships.

## The wider family

One sociological argument of the 1950s ran as follows. Before the industrial revolution in Europe, the predominant family form was extended. That is, people had regular and extensive contact with their wider kin, their grandparents, aunts, uncles and cousins, and they even lived under the same roof. Industrialization, however, changed all that since it entailed substantial migration from the countryside into towns, and as a result people lost contact with their extended family. Families in general shrank to their minimal, nuclear size, consisting of parents and children only. The emotional and personal needs of family members were met within this smaller unit. So, the nuclear family in some sense 'fits' industrial society, while the more extended family is characteristic of pre-industrial society.

This argument is, in many ways, a story of decline and a comparison with a lost golden age – or at least the pessimists discussed earlier in this chapter would think so. I have already indicated in the last chapter that there is some evidence for the appearance of family privatism, of the shrinking of the family. Research in the 1950s and 1960s certainly seemed to show that families no longer had as dense a network of social relationships involving wider family as they had previously. A number of factors were cited as responsible for lessened contact with wider family. Particularly significant are the pressures of work on both men and women, including shift work and flexitime; a greater frequency of moving house which disrupts local social networks, including family; a more instrumental attitude to work so that men and women try to earn as much as possible by working longer hours; and the emergence of a pattern of domesticity in which interests shift to the home and its decoration and improvement, the children and the conjugal tie.

How then has the argument fared against more recent research? Certainly the historical claims look a little bit more shaky. The family in pre-industrial Britain was not extended but consisted largely of relatively small households which were not multi-generational. Furthermore, the industrial revolution did not produce the nuclear family form. Rather the reverse. During the horrors of that period, extended families were actually created in urban centres and acted as protective mutual-aid devices.

The central issue, however, is the extent to which individuals and families are involved with their more distant relatives. The essential conclusion from recent work is that there is still a high degree of involvement as measured by the degree of contact, the flows of support and the emotional importance accorded to wider family, especially on the continuing significance through life of the parent–child tie.

According to one set of recent studies, based on a large sample survey, one-third of adults live within fifteen minutes' travel time of their mother, and no less than 65 per cent live within one hour.[6] This geographical proximity does not, of course, necessarily mean that family members actually see one another. However, it turns out that about half do visit their mother at least once a week and almost three-quarters do so each month. Women, manual workers and, perhaps unsurprisingly, those living nearby will see their mothers particularly often.[7]

If the wider family remains a significant source of social contact for many people, it also continues to function as a form of practical and emotional support. For those who had received practical help, say in times of illness, almost half of that help came from parents and less than 10 per cent from friends. The wider kin network is even more significant in the case of money. Parents were the origin of more than 60 per cent of gifts or loans, with other relatives contributing about 20 per cent. When it comes to flows in the other direction, about two in five of people give care. The most common recipients of care are parents or parents-in-law, who are responsible for about one-third of all care provided. There are some intriguing differences between men and women in the provision of care, for women seem to spread the care that they give out over a wider range of people.

On the face of it, therefore, the story of decline in kinship relationships seems unconvincing. Levels of contact are high, flows of support are robust and vigorous, and people routinely include members of their wider family when asked about their closest social networks. Interestingly, the importance of these relationships survives the disruptions to family life that have become more common in the twenty-first century with the rise in divorce rates and the complexities caused by divorce and the creation of step-families. Wider kinship relationships in turn become very complicated. A parent of an adult child who has divorced may have more than one set of grandchildren. A woman who separates from her partner may potentially end up with more than one network of in-laws. The evidence[8] seems to indicate that kinship systems are sufficiently flexible to encompass these more complex relationships. The pool of kin has become wider and is not based so exclusively on blood ties.

## Local communities and neighbours

The word 'community' carries with it considerable emotive power. Typically, we think of communities – the localities where we live – as good things. Like families they can give security and comfort. They can be a place of daily talk and a source of support and help. As I argued in the first chapter, they can be an important basis for personal identity. They can also have their downsides. They can enforce conformity and restrict freedom. Local gossip can be cruel and undiscriminating and can work to exclude the non-conforming. Neighbours can be intrusive and noisy as well as helpful. Communities – the idea and the reality – therefore embody a tension between security and freedom. Television soap opera, such as *EastEnders* or *Coronation Street*, thrives on precisely that tension.

As so often, the ideal of community is bound up with looking back to a golden age. Frequently, the countryside is the model. The country-side ideal is informed by visual images of various kinds – fields of corn in the sunshine, pretty cottages and contented workers. But there are also assumptions about the way that life is lived, or was lived, in the country. The inhabitants of country communities are assumed to have lived there all their lives and to have married locally. The result is that most people are effectively surrounded by their wider families. Almost everybody works in one occupation – farming. Neighbours are bound together by ties of mutual assistance, whether domestic, as in childcare, or occupa-tional, as in lending each other tools. So, the ideal of community is of a locally based, stable group of people, united by ties of family, tradition and mutual help. To a great extent, such a picture was confirmed by soci-ological research on rural areas of the 1940s and 1950s.[9] Ironically, something of the same picture emerged in studies of inner cities in the same period.[10] These areas housed strong working-class communities also bound together by family ties. Kinship was vital and was maintained by frequent contact and the exchange of services, largely between mothers and adult daughters.

But, in the second half of the twentieth century, the bases for these ideal communities were eroded. Agricultural production has changed. No longer is it a case of producing for local markets by unskilled labour. Relatively skilled agricultural workers do not necessarily work locally but commute or move away. At the same time, the population of rural areas is becoming diversified. Villages are occupied by people who commute to work in towns, by the retired, or those with a second home. Those still in farming seek other sources of income, from tourism, for example. The result is that the country community is very much more diversified and is no longer stable or united by occupation or family. The inner city has changed in some of the same ways. The commercial centre of many cities has expanded outwards, provoking the rebuilding of inner-city residential areas and requiring the rehousing of the inhabitants else-where, thus breaking up long-established communities. The areas left behind can rapidly become slums with a shifting and transitory popula-tion. The inhabitants of the inner city are trapped by poor housing, declining job opportunities, inadequate public services, high rates of vandalism and crime, and deteriorating educational provision with severe teacher shortages. The kind of vicious circle thus developed is not likely to lead to the kinds of attitudes and behaviour described in the ideal of community. If the inhabitants of the inner city stay there, it is only because they cannot leave.

Social changes of this kind, then, have often led to a belief that the virtues of communities of the past, allegedly exemplified in the inner city and the countryside, have disappeared. According to popular myth, neighbours are no longer helpful people who have lived there a long time and who will lend a ladder, mind the children or help at hay-making. Instead, at the very best, neighbours are invisible, shadowy people who have no sooner arrived than they have moved on elsewhere. At the worst, they are suspicious, nosy, noisy, or even violently aggressive. This view of the community finds its way into television and film, which often use the suburb to represent the decline of community as a network of supportive relationships. The television series *One Foot in the Grave*, for instance, portrays neighbourly relationships in the suburb as hostile or eccentric. The film *American Beauty* depicts suburban life in America as tawdry and unfulfilling and beset by murderous neighbours.

Again, to an extent, earlier sociological work confirmed aspects of this myth. Thus, Michael Young and Peter Wilmott, the authors of the study of the inner city mentioned earlier, which found there a sense of community based in a kinship network, also carried out an investigation of a suburban council housing estate to which many inhabitants of the inner city were being rehoused.[11] Young and Wilmott took the view that the move from the inner city to a suburban location represented a loss of community. An important reason for this was that it naturally severed the network of supportive relationships based in the wider family, work and friendship that had been built up over so many years. As significant as this, however, was the development of a novel style of life very different from that in the inner city and one which is not simply the product of a move to unfamiliar territory. The family turns inwards, becomes more involved in domestic matters, and husband and wife are more emotionally bound up with each other and their children – a style of life described in the last chapter as family privatism. The result is a changed attitude to the neighbours and the neighbourhood. Although personal contact is minimal, people feel the presence of their neighbours, not as helpful and friendly as they had in the inner city, but, rather, as potentially hostile.

The proposition is, then, that the ideal of community, as an active network of supportive personal relationships, is more nearly realized the more that the social ties of family, work, friendship and neighbours overlap and reinforce each other. The early twenty-first century seems to be a time when people move house frequently (about 10 per cent move each year) and increasingly keep their social ties in separate compartments. In these circumstances, what are relationships with neighbours actually like? Are they in the active circle of people we talk to?

Most people make a distinction between neighbours and friends. A study of the way in which the elderly secured support found that older people distinguished friends, who might not live close by but could be counted on to provide extensive and long-term help, and neighbours, who happened to live nearby and would provide assistance in an emergency even if that meant that they went to get one of the friends. The degree to which neighbours will be counted as friends will, however, vary, and this may well be because of differing interpretations of the word 'friend'. As we saw in the previous chapter, working-class respondents will be hesitant in using the word and, in practice, have a conception of friendship that is very context-dependent. The middle class, on the other hand, have a more generalizable notion of friendship. Middle-class people, therefore, may be more inclined to identify neighbours as friends. Another study by Young and Wilmott, this time of a middle-class suburb, noted that a network of friends replaced the wider family as the basis of community sentiment.[12] This network mostly came from the surrounding twenty or thirty houses and could be a group with between two and a dozen members. Outside this group were the other local residents – 'neighbours' with whom there were friendly relations although they were not friends.

Friends, however, are not necessarily *close* friends with whom one is intimate in the sense discussed in the previous chapter. If asked about the truly intimate circle of friends and family, most people will recognize close friends, but those do not, on the whole, live in the locality. One recent study found that people would identify, on average, about five friends in their street but only one close friend. The elderly were more likely to find best friends in the immediate neighbourhood.[13] It is almost as if some physical distance was required in order to maintain really close friendship – except, perhaps, for the elderly.

A distinction between friends and neighbours does not mean that there are not friendly relationships with neighbours, just that they are different kinds of social relationship. Any tendency to family privatism or greater individualization of the kind described in the previous chapter does not mean that local community relations die out altogether. Although abrasive relationships between neighbours receive a lot of publicity, actually those relationships tend to be much more easy-going and cooperative than the myth would indicate. Neighbours exchange small favours readily – feeding plants or animals, baby-sitting, taking in parcels, for instance. Those who live nearby oil the wheels of daily life. As a respondent in one study said:

> The neighbour next door, I get her shopping, and if it's a wet day I'll
> go and get her paper ... when she was able to, when we went on

holiday she used to look after the house . . . She used to water our greenhouse for us, that sort of thing. And also she used to babysit my daughter . . . when she was young.[14]

It is true that there will also be daily irritations, with noise or parking, for instance. When asked, however, most people will note such incidents but add that they are trivial. Crucially, neighbourly relations are a balance between offering and receiving help when it is needed with respect for family privacy. People want to achieve reciprocity in small favours but they do not necessarily want an oppressive relationship which might disturb their household. This 'friendly distance' is a difficult balance to strike and requires careful management.

## Associations

Friendships, contacts with wider family, and community ties do not account for all of an individual's personal relationships outside of the immediate family and work. Many people are involved in a whole range of organizations that may take up a considerable amount of time and energy. The critical question to be answered is: does membership of voluntary organizations, attendance at evening classes, participation in hobbies and pastimes necessarily involve people in a network of supportive social relationships, and is this kind of activity diminishing?

Voluntary organizations have been part of the British social landscape for a very long time. In that time, some organizations have declined and others have grown in membership. Thus, the membership of many traditional and women's organizations has fallen during the post-war period. For example, between 1971 and 1990, the Mothers' Union declined from 308,000 members to 177,000, the National Union of Townswomen's Guilds from 216,000 to 105,000, and the women's section of the Royal British Legion from 162,000 to 105,000. On the other hand, in the same period, organizations broadly to do with the environment increased in membership. The National Trust, for example, had 278,000 members in 1971 but more than 2 million in 1995; the membership of the Royal Society for the Protection of Birds rose from 98,000 to 890,000, while that of the World Wildlife Fund for Nature moved from 12,000 to 219,000. Despite variations of this kind, overall it is likely that there is growth in membership of voluntary organizations that exceeds population growth. One estimate is that the average number of memberships per person was 1.12 in 1990 compared with 0.73 in 1959.[15] In the late 1990s about one-quarter of the population had been involved in voluntary activity of some kind although, for many, that activity did not take up much time.[16] Of course, simple membership may not be a very good guide to the *meaning* of the activity for the participant. Many of the newer organizations only involve paying a membership fee rather than actually *doing* anything in concert with others. There is not enough evidence yet that changes in participation in voluntary organizations have also involved change in the nature of the social networks formed.

With other kinds of organizations it is clearer that participation brings with it a set of social relationships. Many people, for instance, are involved in enthusiasms – hobbies, pastimes, leisure pursuits – undertaken collectively with others in clubs or societies. There is a huge variety of enthusiasms, ranging from soccer to the keeping of tropical fish, from model railways to dress-making, and from stamp-collecting to the rearing of fancy rats. Any visit to a large newsagent will demonstrate the extent and diversity of enthusiasms from the number of magazines on sale. One study of enthusiasms found that, in one area of Bristol, there were at least 300 groups of enthusiasts of various kinds, with an average membership of ninety, out of a population of 85,000 people.[17] These groups were often well established and long-lived; one-half had been running for over fifteen years. Although these are leisure activities, many of the participants bring professional standards to their involvement. Enthusiasms, therefore, involve skills that are practised in the enthusiasm itself – being knowledgeable about tropical fish or being dextrous in the modelling of railway locomotives. They also demand the development of standards of judgement of the contributions made by the participants, standards which almost inevitably imply competition. At the same time, enthusiasms are *social*, involving mutual aid and reciprocity, even when the activity itself, as in the case of gardening, is not an intrinsically collective activity.

The same qualities of social participation, collective endeavour and the deployment of skill and knowledge are characteristic of other kinds of activity. Here, for example, is a journalist describing the Barry Manilow fan club:

> What is it about Barry Manilow? Apart from the hype and gross sentimentality and general rubbish, what else is it that makes it different from any other hysterical crowd scene? It is not Barry Manilow himself, that is for sure. He is a bad singer of banal songs. It is his following, not him, that is special . . . The promise Manilow puts out in his songs is that if you love him, your life will change. From being lonely, unappreciated, a misfit in society, you will find a kindred soul and achieve that Barryapotheosis of being lonely together. The odd thing is that, in a way, the promise is fulfilled. I talked to dozens of

women who had been stuck at home, depressed, friendless, prospect-less, when they first heard Manilow's music. They dreamt that Barry would come through the door and make everything right. He didn't. But what happened instead was that they joined their local fan club, met like-minded sentimentalists, shared their problems, attended Barrybashes, set off to conventions, concerts, and places they never would have believed they could reach: in short their lives *were* changed, and for the better.[18]

There is a tendency to regard fan clubs as refuges for obsessive or hys-terical people who have no lives of their own. Such a view neglects the way in which such groups provide a network of social relationships – social capital – and allow members to develop skills in collective activity.

Two studies of fan clubs organized around television programmes of the 1970s and 1980s illustrate the point.[19] People have formed fan groups around a variety of television shows, including *Star Trek, Blake's 7, The Professionals, Starsky and Hutch* and *Doctor Who*. The interest in the television series occupies a substantial part of the fans' time and they will meet with others to view the series concerned, to attend meet-ings and full-scale conventions, and, above all, to engage actively with the medium in a variety of different ways.

Fans are organized in different ways, formally and informally. They may meet fairly frequently in small local groups in each other's houses (in 'circles'). Rather more formally, local clubs may be formed which are dedicated to a particular show. Even more formally, conventions are held regularly all over the country, and abroad, which may attract from fifty to 10,000 fans. At the same time, there are a large number of fanzines to which the fans contribute, which again vary in their degree of organ-ization, from several photocopied sheets to larger, and more profession-ally produced, publications.

These fan groups are not passive viewers of television material. Using the characters in the programmes of which they were fans, they wrote stories, plays and poetry, composed songs, drew portraits, made cos-tumes, created photographs from video, designed jewellery, pottery or needlework, published books or fanzines, devised indexes and cata-logues, and wrote essays of criticism. The stories could be of several dif-ferent forms. One type focused on *Star Trek*, for example, involves a woman as a heroine who saves the *Enterprise* but dies in the attempt. Another type is built around the supposition that Captain Kirk and Mr Spock have a sexual relationship. Almost any type of story is possible. Alternative universe stories, for example, put characters from one pro-gramme in a quite different universe. In one, for example, Ray Doyle from *The Professionals* becomes an elf. Many of the resulting stories are collective products in which a whole fan community develops the plot over time, interweaving the story itself with illustrations, poems and songs. Story trees arise in which one story builds on another using the same characters. The most important point stressed by the authors of these studies is that fans are very far from being passive consumers of television programmes. Quite the contrary: they are extremely active in transforming what they watch and they are social in all they do. The fan groups are partly about forming social relationships with others.

## Social networks and social health

It is obvious that nearly everybody is involved in a network of personal relationships. That network will provide, in varying degrees, love, emotional support, friendship and practical help. One way of conceiving of the structure of personal networks is as a set of concentric circles radiating out from the individual. In the inner circle, most people place members of their family and their very closest friends. Relationships with these are characterized by the intimacy that I discussed in the last chapter. It is the circles further out that I have been discussing in this chapter, the relationships with wider family and friends, both in the community and in organizations of various kinds. The issue raised at the beginning of the chapter was whether this wider personal network is robust.

On the whole, my argument has been that wider relationships of this kind function well. So, despite the stories that appear in the media of the decline of the wider family and the neglect of the elderly or of the collapse of neighbourly relationships, actually, for most people, the networks of relationships with elderly parents or aunts and uncles and with those who live nearby are alive and well. Of course, the density or extent of personal networks – the volume of social capital – is variable. Individuals will have networks of very different sizes. Different social groups will organize networks in different ways. For example, as I have already indicated, members of the middle class tend to have a larger network of friends than do members of the working class. They also tend to be involved to a greater extent in voluntary organizations of all kinds, which gives them access to a network of contacts. In this sense, the middle class will have more social capital. Similarly, ethnic minorities, particularly those who originated from the Indian sub-continent, can form localized communities in which there are dense networks of family and friends. Such communities are very similar to the working-class communities of the 1950s that I discussed earlier in the chapter and, like them, are formed as mechanisms of defence and mutual support in an uncertain and potentially hostile world.

In asking if the network of personal relationships in the United Kingdom is robust, however, a convincing study would have to look at the development of networks over time. Is the social capital available to the inhabitants of the United Kingdom being attenuated?

Some evidence which might help us to answer that question is provided by a study comparing the degree of contact with wider family in 1995 with that in 1986.[20] One might first note that, the younger the person, the less likely it is that they will be family-centred. Thus, four in ten of 18- to 34-year-olds agree that people should keep in contact with wider family, compared with just over half of those aged between 35 and 44 and two-thirds of those over 55. Neither does the presence of dependent children make a difference. These data indicate that attitudes, and perhaps behaviour, are becoming less favourable to involvement with relatives, although one should bear in mind that another interpretation is that people simply become more family-centred as they age.

Overall, levels of contact with relatives and friends have fallen in those ten years. Those with dependent children having weekly contact with their mothers has fallen from 59 per cent in 1986 to 50 per cent in 1995. The fall is greater among those with children under five, a result that is consistent with the changes in attitudes to wider family involvement described above. This change is partly the result of an increasing geographical separation between relatives, but, even after taking this into account, the decline in contact is still there.

Closer analysis shows even more striking changes. While both men and women see less of their relatives, for full-time employed women the change is dramatic. In 1986, two-thirds of this category saw their mother weekly. By 1995, this proportion had declined to under half and is now roughly the same as for full-time employed men. This suggests that the nature of women's work has changed over the last ten years and has become more demanding, leaving less time and energy for seeing relatives. Alternatively, women are now entering the labour market who have changed attitudes and attach a greater priority to work than did their predecessors. There are social class changes of similar magnitude. Over the last decade there has been a drop of 19 percentage points in the proportion of non-manual workers seeing their mothers once a week, while there has been little change for manual workers. These appear to be striking changes. However, this is not really a long enough period of time to make a conclusive judgement, and there may have been circumstances special to the late 1980s and early 1990s.

There is other evidence that appears to show that there has *not* been a general decline in the density or extent of personal networks. For example, one study[21] compared the personal networks of older people in three urban areas with those studied some fifty years earlier in the same locations. The methodology does not allow precise comparison, but the authors conclude that elderly people in these three areas continue to have significant networks of people living fairly close by who can support them in times of need. Those networks are dominated by family members, especially children, although friends tend to be relatively more important in suburban locations where kinship is more fragmented. Nonetheless, the authors concede that the network is more geographically stretched as children or other family have moved away. And elderly people tend to live now in smaller households consisting of one or two people, whereas fifty years ago their households would have had children or lodgers in them as well (Bangladeshi families being a notable exception).

In the United States, by contrast, the position may be clearer. One large study of networks of personal relationships in America by Robert Putnam concludes that the stock of social capital built up in the first half of the twentieth century is being substantially dissipated.[22] Political participation has dropped, whether that is expressed in voting, knowledge of public affairs, working for political parties, running for office or even signing of petitions. Furthermore, the decline is sharpest in such cooperative activities as helping parties in elections and slowest in relatively passive activities, say, letter-writing. Similarly, civic participation, those activities that I have earlier described in terms of belonging to voluntary organizations, has also deteriorated. Although membership of some organizations may well have increased in America, this vigour is really restricted to mailing-list organizations. Those that depend on local *activity* are in decline.

America has always been thought of as a religious country, certainly by comparison with Northern Europe. Indeed, half of all personal philanthropy, and half of all volunteering, is religious in character. Those people who are active members of their religious community are also those who are most active politically and civically. However, religion is becoming less important. In the last twenty-five years, attendance at acts of worship has declined by about 10 per cent, and the trend appears to be accelerating. It might be argued that, as work has become more central to the everyday lives of Americans, so also have the social relationships with work colleagues, which contribute a kind of social capital. However, when asked who their most important social contacts are, most Americans do not cite workmates. In fact, neighbours appear more frequently in the list than colleagues. In addition, changes in the nature of work have had an impact on the intimacy or supportiveness of relationships in the workplace. There is more outsourcing of jobs, the intensity of work has increased, and the idea of a stable career with one employer is disappearing. These changes are more likely to make the relationships at work rather more competitive than cooperative.

So far, most of the social relationships described derive effectively from membership in formal organizations. What about informal contacts, such as having people in for a drink, playing cards, or going to the cinema with others? Here also there is decline. Americans are spending less time in social contacts with neighbours and friends and more time in watching rather than doing. Simple conversation is being increasingly avoided.

Putnam's conclusion is a depressing one. There has been a remarkably consistent decline in social capital across so many areas of human activity. Multi-stranded networks, in which each person is embedded in dense webs where all participants interact with each other in several different ways, are being replaced by single-stranded ones in which the participants interact in only one way. His study concedes that there may be some counter-tendencies. The apparent growth in self-help groups and in communication by telephone and email may counter the loss of social capital, but these are not enough to make up the losses.

Putnam identifies a number of causes of the decline in social capital. It is often said that work has become more demanding and that restricts the ability to exercise personal networks. It is not altogether clear that work has *in general* taken up more time and energy. However, one of the most significant social changes of the last fifty years has been the increase in the numbers of women in employment, and it has largely been women who organized the networks that contribute to social capital. Putnam notes that full-time work for women cuts volunteering by 50 per cent, and the effect is even stronger for those who work because they have to rather than because they want to. Second, changes in the places where people live have had an effect. There has been an increasing flight to the sprawling suburbs in which communities are very homogeneous in social composition, a factor which is known to decrease the size and scope of networks. In addition, a greater suburbanization increases the time that people spend commuting – alone – by car. Every ten minutes extra spent in commuting time cuts involvement in community affairs by 10 per cent. Of greater significance still for Putnam is the increasing tendency for people to take their leisure in the home (an aspect of the social privatism discussed in the last chapter). Television here is the chief culprit, in that it consumes a lot of time and it encourages a passivity. Lastly, and most importantly, is a generational change. Putnam finds that successive generations born since the Second World War are increasingly materialistic and decreasingly community-orientated, a finding that he attributes to the effect of world wars in instilling a consciousness of the community.[23]

In sum, the evidence for a decline in the intensity and extent of personal networks is more equivocal for Britain than the United States.

Though relationships with wider family appeared to be flourishing, very recent evidence may suggest a decline in the degree of contact. Contemporary myths about neighbours are largely misleading. Neighbours are generally willing to help in domestic matters, although they are probably not close friends. Other kinds of relationship in the community, participation in voluntary organizations, for example, continue to draw in many people, although the quality of participation may be altering.

But, to return finally to the questions posed at the beginning of the chapter, why should it matter? An increase in individualism or family privatism at the expense of wider social networks may have social advantages, especially in terms of greater freedom for individuals. But there are also significant drawbacks. To take but one example, those who have less social capital, a less developed personal network, are not only at greater risk of suicide but are generally less healthy and are less well supported when ill. Indeed, it may be that social order itself is dependent on the social relationships outside the family, since that is how family units are knit together. That is an issue to which I return later in the book.

# 5

# Is work a curse?

It is impossible to enjoy idling thoroughly unless one has plenty of work to do.

Jerome K. Jerome

In contemporary societies, many people find work a curse. Some have not got enough of it. For others it is too badly paid. A lot of people work very long hours and resent it. For many that are reasonably paid and in relatively continuous employment, work is nevertheless a source of stress and anxiety. Still others think that work is a tedious necessity that prevents them from getting on with their real lives which occupy their leisure time. This distinction is the stuff of so many modern day-dreams encouraged by films, television, magazines and advertising. People look forward to the end of the day, Friday and the weekend, and holidays as time free of work. More radically, they will dream of winning the lottery and not having to work at all. In the dream, work is seen as constraining, limiting, dull, grinding and boring; leisure, on the other hand, represents choice, freedom, fun and pleasure.

However, the relationship with work is not a simple one. Quite a few of those who work long hours appear to enjoy it. Very many people find in their work a source of companionship, involvement in collective endeavour, and social status, as well as money. Many, indeed, find it difficult to occupy their leisure time and are even more at a loss in retirement. For almost everybody, though, work, or perhaps its absence or anticipation, is a major part of life.

## What is work?

A lot of different kinds of activities are called work. Both bankers and bus drivers will talk about their work. A student will say to her friends that she is going off to work when she means that she has an essay to write. A retired person speaks of going to work at a voluntary organization where he regularly puts in a day per week. A woman at home may talk of house*work*. Many hobbies and pastimes, gardening for instance, often look like work. These activities are all work in the sense that they are undertaken with a purpose, using a skill of some kind, often in concert with others, transforming the world in some way, however small, and usually having an output which can be used by other people, whether it is a good or a service.

Many people in modern societies, of course, also make a distinction between *paid* work and leisure. For the practical purposes of everyday life this appears to be a distinction that everybody can appreciate. Looked at closely, however, it is rather muddy. If a large company gives corporate hospitality at a major sporting event and expects its employees to make useful contacts with guests, then paid work and leisure appear to be inseparable both for those employees and their guests. More significantly, different societies will define the division between paid work and leisure differently. In pre-industrial societies, for example, human labour was rather more task-orientated in that people worked to accomplish a particular task, such as ploughing a field. They did not work for a given period of time and then turn to leisure. In the absence of measurement of work by the clock, work was not easily distinguished from merely passing the time of day.[1] The meaning of work, in other words, is not fixed but is socially constructed.

In contrast with earlier conceptions, the modern notion of work posits a distinction between paid work, undertaken for an agreed period of time each day or week, for an agreed amount of money, and leisure, which is time free of such work and under each person's control. With work and leisure understood in this way, the supply of leisure time in Britain has risen gradually over the last century. For example, manual workers in most industries worked an average of more than fifty-five hours per week at the beginning of the century. This had fallen to fifty hours by 1943 and less than forty-three by 1985. The average hours worked by the population as a whole fell steadily throughout the 1980s and in 1991 stood at rather less than thirty-six hours per week. To look at it from the other side, it has been estimated that the total amount of leisure time available to the British population rose by an average of 0.5 per cent per year from 1982 to 1992.[2] However, the British still have longer working days by quite a margin than their continental European counterparts. Furthermore, there are signs that this trend to increased leisure time slackened in the 1990s. In addition, there are other changes in work patterns that are concealed by taking simple averages of hours worked. There are greater differences in work hours, with some people working longer hours and others shorter. At the same time, there has been an increase over the last thirty years in the proportion of households in which nobody works. Again, the pattern of work may make it less easy to make use of any leisure time, particularly if leisure pursuits involve others. It is no longer quite so true that everybody works a standard working day. Thus, one in six employees now works in the evening and one in two working men and one in three working women work for some or all of Sunday.

Of course, some people do not have the luxury of a contrast between paid work and leisure, in that they are unemployed. The rate of unemployment fluctuates over time. For some thirty years after the end of the Second World War, on average about 3 per cent of the workforce was unemployed. There was a rapid rise in the 1980s, reaching a peak of 12 per cent, and then a decline to about 5 per cent towards the end of the century. There is a common conception that those who are unemployed have been so for some time and there is therefore a pool of the intractably long-term unemployed. Actually, only about one half of people unemployed at any one time are still unemployed one year later. Unfortunately, those who have been unemployed are more likely to have spells of unemployment later. There may well be a pool, but it is of people who move in and out of unemployment. A further point, which will be developed in the next chapter, is critical to the understanding of unemployment. A concentration on the unemployment of *individuals* is misleading because unemployment is becoming increasingly concentrated in households or families. In 1975, about 4 per cent of *households* were workless. By 1995, that had risen to 15 per cent.[3] In some households, therefore, both partners are unemployed. So also are their sons and daughters, and part of the reason for that is that youth unemployment has risen sharply over the past three or four decades.

If work may be a curse, *not* having it is worse. A large proportion of those who are unemployed live in poverty, and the longer the unemployment lasts, the deeper the poverty. Even those who go in and out of unemployment do not travel particularly far up the income ladder when they are employed. This means a condition of mere existence, cutting back on food, clothes, holidays, social activities, household repairs, for instance. The unemployed are less healthy physically and mentally. They are more prone to divorce. They are also more socially isolated, cut off from social contact at work but also unable to make other contacts because of lack of money. They lose status among wider family and friends and their self-confidence and sense of self-worth declines sharply. The following quotation from a man interviewed in a study of unemployment illustrates just part of the experience:

> It affected me a lot when I was unemployed. I didn't think I was going to get another job. It was very depressing and got worse the longer I was unemployed. It wasn't so much the money or the way I felt. It was degrading – in the dole office or when people asked me what I was doing . . . When you are unemployed, you are bored, frustrated, and worried sick: at least I was.[4]

## The organization of work

Most people work in an organization of some kind. At the same time, the press is full of stories of the changing pattern of work. We hear of the growth of portfolio careers, self-employment and working from home. Many celebrate the freedom from organizational life that this is said to bring. However, even the self-employed (12 per cent of the workforce) or those who work from home (3 per cent) are necessarily involved in the systems and procedures of the companies or institutions that they do work for.

Most work organizations will have relatively formal structures and rules, which may be codified in documents. One way of describing these structures is to use the idea of bureaucracy. On the whole, bureaucracies do not attract favourable comment. They are often seen as crushing of innovation, full of red tape, time-wasting and impersonal – in short, bureaucratic. Thus, Charles Dickens in *Little Dorrit*, writing in the nineteenth century, describes the working of a fictional government office, which he christened the Circumlocution Office, like this:

> If another Gunpowder Plot had been discovered half an hour before the lighting of the match, no-body would have been justified in saving the parliament until there had been half a score of boards, half a bushel of minutes, several sacks of official memoranda and a family-vault full of ungrammatical correspondence, on the part of the Circumlocution Office.[5]

However, bureaucratic organization can also be efficient. The classical account of bureaucracy[6] suggests that there are five important elements in its operation. First, bureaucracy depends on a system of *rules*. Bureaucrats do not, in other words, act arbitrarily or on a whim but in accordance with a set of rules which therefore preclude the necessity for specific instructions in each case. Second, bureaucracies are hierarchies. They have a command structure in which senior officials control junior ones. The hierarchy is legitimated by belief in the correctness of the rules. The bureaucrat is loyal to a superior *position* rather than to the *person* who holds it. Third, the relationship between bureaucrats and their clients is an impersonal one. Bureaucrats do not change their behaviour for particular people but apply the rules impersonally. Of course, it is just this impersonality that upsets people who come across bureaucracies. In treating everybody impersonally, individuals seem to be robbed of their personal identity and circumstances, which they may believe entitles them to individual treatment. Fourth, bureaucrats are appointed on the basis of their ability and technical knowledge. It is not *who* they know that is important but *what* they know.

Fifth, each bureaucratic official is highly specialized but has a limited area of responsibility and discretion. Most work processes in modern societies have a high degree of *division of labour*. The processes are split up into smaller and smaller steps, each of which becomes more specialized. The classical example is the production line on which cars are manufactured. The cars move past the workers each of whom has a particular task to perform. One may be fitting boot lids, another tightening nuts. This is an efficient means of producing cars because each worker becomes very adept at the small range of tasks he or she performs. It is also possible to reduce wage rates because someone capable of carrying out a small task will be paid less than a highly skilled craftsman who might be able to build the whole car.

It is possible to design almost all work processes in this way. Manufacturing processes are the obvious example, but office work also is easily split up into component steps. Even professional and service work can be treated in the same way. In accountants' and lawyers' practices, for example, there is constant pressure to redefine categories of work so that less well-paid assistants carry out routine work. In turn, the partners take to specializing in particular areas. Similarly in medicine, nurses are moving more into the more routine aspects of consultation and prescribing.

In describing the bureaucratic organization of work so far I have very much been presenting an abstract, idealized picture. Do bureaucratic organizations actually work like that in the real world? Are the formal rules and procedures actually followed?

In fact, no organization could operate if the formal bureaucratic rules *were* rigorously adhered to. The formal rules may be impossible to implement in changing circumstances, they may make operations far too slow, and they may contradict each other. The obsessive rule-following that is so often supposed to be characteristic of bureaucrats will mean that the ultimate aims of the organization are forgotten and applying the rules becomes an end in itself. The result is that a set of informal practices grow up among the employees to enable them to do their jobs at all and to fulfil the aims of the organization. One illustration of this point is the practice of working to rule, now less common than formerly. If employees are disgruntled with particular management proposals, one strategy that they can employ is to follow the rules that regulate their workplace *very* precisely. If, for example, the rules prescribe that two people have to be present for a particular procedure, they will insist that the rule is obeyed slavishly. The result is that work is done very slowly. In other words, it is only by ignoring or bending organizational rules that anything gets done.

Employees, therefore, can make the system work by ignoring the rules – and can paralyse it by following them. Every organization develops an *informal* culture which enables everybody to get through the day. That culture is not articulated or written down. But everybody knows how it works. It is regulated and produced by the kinds of processes discussed in chapter 1; infringements are subtly punished and conformity rewarded without fanfare. And this informal culture has consequences well beyond simply making bureaucracies work, because the formal rules cannot anticipate every contingency. This point is aptly illustrated by a study of the implicit moral codes that inform the activities of managers in large companies in the United States.[7]

The companies studied were certainly hierarchical. They had complex grading systems that formally allocated people to positions in the hierarchy. Every manager knew his or her place. Furthermore, behaviour was dictated by the views of bosses. However, this was not an impersonal issue. For the managers concerned, it very much mattered who their boss was – and what whims, opinions and fixations that boss had. A great deal of effort was expended in trying to anticipate likely instructions or even unexpressed wishes. As one manager said:

> The whole informal body of knowledge is a crucial set of maps to the organization. It helps you gauge how you relate to others – what you can and can't do. And this knowledge and the relationships ebb and flow. Sometimes a guy is nonpromotable today and tomorrow he is the very best man. Everything depends on who is on top and how he perceives you and other people.[8]

The life of a manager, in other words, is very far from the impersonal model of the classical account of bureaucracy. It is a world in which not only is there a personal relationship with a superior, but it is also necessary to be able to trust colleagues with whom one is involved in joint projects. Within large organizations alliances are crucial and personal qualities paramount:

> One becomes known, for instance, as a trusted friend of a friend; thought of as a person to whom one can safely refer a thorny problem; considered a 'sensible' or 'reasonable' or, especially, a 'flexible' person, not a 'renegade' or a 'loose cannon rolling around the lawn'; known to be a discreet person attuned to the nuances of corporate etiquette, one who can keep one's mouth shut . . .[9]

In a world of personal relationships, governed by an understood and inexplicit culture, managers have to look out for themselves. It is essential to have a patron who will help the junior manager to show off his or her abilities. Blame has to be shifted and risky decisions avoided. Such a culture will encourage behaviour likely to lead to present advantage but which may cost a good deal more in the future. Managers in the study, therefore, described the practice of milking cash from a manufacturing plant without putting in any investment, thus generating healthy profits. As a result of apparent success, the people involved would receive promotion and would not therefore be around when the lack of investment caused major losses. Or, senior managers kept profits in line with targets by transferring money in and out of the employees' pension funds, an extremely risky, if familiar, procedure.

The point is, of course, that all these activities seem entirely natural to the managers themselves. This is simply how they do their jobs, how they do what they are asked to do. Their everyday world of work is paramount. If challenged, the managers did not exhibit shame or remorse, even when what they did might endanger the health of workers or customers. Rather, they were puzzled that objections might be raised. This is what makes the public outrage that greeted the corporate scandals of 2002 involving Enron and Worldcom and others somewhat ironic. Behaviour of this kind is *normal* in large organizations.

Organizations are fundamentally about control. They are devices for organizing human labour and technology in the pursuit of a set of aims, profit, military victory, or delivery of welfare benefit, for instance. This implies that one group of people has the power to direct the activities of another group. The result is that there is always a potential conflict of interest between employers and employees, and the latter may resent and resist control. Some forms of resistance are formal and parallel the explicit organizational structure. Thus, trade unions will be formed to represent the interests of workers and negotiate with management. In pursuit of those interests, from time to time, unions will organize strikes to try to force management to change some policy. Since the late 1970s in the United Kingdom, however, these mechanisms have been in decline. In 1979 there were some 12 million trade union members, but by the late 1990s this had fallen to under 8 million. Strike activity has also become far less prominent. In 1977, 448 working days per 1000 employees were lost through industrial stoppages. By 1997, this had fallen to a mere ten.[10]

Official forms of protest are, however, only the most obvious kinds of resistance. Hidden, informal resistance can be much more effective day to day. The development of an informal culture can be used to make the organization work more effectively, but it can also be employed to disrupt. In one study of a clothing factory,[11] for example, the women on the shop floor formed an informal culture that was practically *defined* by its resistance to management. It was a culture united by friendships that continued outside the factory and by a conviction that one had to get through the day by treating the job partly as a laugh. The women therefore directed a stream of jokes, some at each other, but most at the representatives of management, especially if they were men whose sexual prowess would be impugned. Theirs was a never-ending attempt to create time and space of their own, free from management supervision. Thus, the women would bring in sewing jobs of their own that needed doing and use the company's materials and equipment. They would set off fire alarms, jam machines, spend too long in the coffee room, or deliberately go slow in production or packing. All these are methods used in so many workplaces by employees wishing to resist management demands, to relieve tension and frustration, or just to get through the day. Sabotage, for example, is not typically the action of a lone, dissident employee but is much more commonly collectively *organized*. Here are two examples from a study of industrial sabotage:

> An unofficial campaign in New York by film projectionists was successful in securing a new two-year contract and a 15 per cent rise in wages by startling audiences with films shown upside down, alarming noises from the sound machines, mixing reels from other films and showing films on the ceiling instead of the screen.

> Our research at the carpet factory revealed a common practice of standing at the back of the looms and pulling out ends. This meant that the weaver had to stop the loom to mend it; meanwhile the other workers gained a break. Our informant told us that one could calculate exactly how long the loom would be stopped . . .[12]

Above all, however, there was resistance around the method of payment. The women were set targets of the numbers of completed items to be produced in a given time. Management decided those targets by measuring the time taken to finish a garment. This produced a straightforward conflict of interest. It was in the management's interest to set higher targets and thereby to reduce costs. It was in the women's interest to slow up the labour process, lower the targets and maximize their wages. Every time a target was set, the workers would object. Frequently, they would down tools and nothing at all would be done. As a result, the targets that were set were actually a compromise between the needs of management and the resistance offered by the women. It is important to note that this is not just about wages; it is also about control. The workers experienced the system of payment as a severe restriction on their personal freedom.

## Changing work

People sometimes look back on the 1950s, 1960s and 1970s as a golden age of work. It is true that films of the period do not often depict work in any detail. But when they do, the impression that we get is of a fairly leisurely work life, predictable and assured, with lifelong careers in the same industry or even enterprise, and little unemployment. Husbands work full-time until they retire and wives largely stay at home and care for the children.

Contrast that image of the organization of work with that depicted in films made towards the end of the century, such as *Working Girl* or *Wall Street*. In both of these films women work and have careers. But they do not make things; they deliver services. Work is depicted here as being frenzied. By contrast with the leisurely pace of films of the 1950s, everyone seems to be running. The world is changing very quickly, throwing up business opportunities that have to be grasped in a moment. Rewards may be high but so too is the risk of failure. Mistakes are likely to be punished instantly with the sack. Neither is this picture restricted to fictional presentations. We are frequently being told by politicians and journalists that the world of work is changing and society must adapt. Workforces have to be more skilled. People must be prepared to change career more often. Workers will have to undertake a variety of tasks rather than concentrating on a few. There will be more working from home. More people will earn their living by acting as freelancers or by working at more than one job at the same time.

How accurate an image of modern work is this?

First, there has apparently been a shift in the economies of the northern half of the world from manufacturing to the delivery of services. In the United Kingdom in 1951, about 5 per cent of the working population was employed in the primary sector (industries such as mining or agriculture), 50 per cent in the secondary sector (car or television production) and 45 per cent in the tertiary sector (services such as tourism or catering). Towards the end of the century, the primary sector was almost unchanged, but the secondary sector had shrunk to under 20 per cent, with the tertiary sector employing almost 80 per cent of the workforce.[13] Care should be taken in interpreting these data, however. Employment in manufacturing may have fallen but its output has actually risen. This is because the extensive use of machines has greatly raised productivity per employee and the organization of production has become more efficient. The distinction between services and manufacturing is, furthermore, less clear than might be expected. Much service employment, in transport, for instance, is only there because goods are manufactured. Similarly, catering may be defined as a service, but it actually involves manufacturing meals.

The growth in service employment is often celebrated as a release of workers from dull, dangerous, unhealthy manufacturing jobs. It is claimed that service workers are more skilled, involved in more interesting and varied jobs, and work in clean, quiet and safe environments. How likely is such a claim?

Eating out has become much more common than it was fifty years ago. Visits to restaurants are not restricted to occasional celebrations but may be regular events in the leisure timetable.[14] Quite often this may be little more than a substitute for the family meal and is the replacement by a service industry of something that we previously did ourselves. But also quite often it is rather more of a serious event than that. Doubtless a little of this eating out involves the deployment of great skill by chefs who have had long periods of apprenticeship and training. Indeed, cooking at a high level is currently being regarded as an art form. Some chefs are treated as celebrities, invited to host television programmes and write cookery books. Catering at this level, in other words, is attended by considerable glamour. But the great bulk of the catering industry is nothing like that. It is essentially an industrialized process operated by workers who are badly paid and relatively unskilled. In the great majority of catering outlets, whether they are providing fast food at lunch times or in the evening, or are in schools, hospitals or workplaces, most employees are acting as kitchen porters or cleaners or are serving customers. These are unskilled occupations. Much of the food is pre-prepared in standardized portions and is cooked by machine. Those who are involved in the preparation and cooking are participating in a work process which is split into a number of stages, each of which involves little or no skill. Here is a catering worker talking about her work:

It's just like a factory making radios. It *is* a factory. When we prepare the food, we don't think that someone is going to sit down and enjoy it. As long as it looks all right we are not making any effort to improve the quality. There is no variety . . . everything by the book, always the same way.[15]

There is a movement from manufacturing to services, therefore, but it may not have the impact on the experiences of workers that has been thought. A second change, this time of the organization of work of all kinds, may be more significant. The contrast here is between bureaucratic and more flexible forms of work. The former – often called Fordism after Henry Ford, the car maker who pioneered that form of manufacturing – as we have seen, involves fragmenting the processes of work into separate stages, each of which requires workers to specialize, mass production and a centralized management. The product range is limited by the method of production; Henry Ford famously said that his customers could have any colour of car as long as it was black.

Flexible systems, on the other hand, allow employers to respond to volatile, more competitive and more differentiated markets. A number of features are associated with such systems. First, in earlier chapters, I described a tendency for contemporary societies to put increased stress on the individual and on choice in lifestyles. The result is a much greater diversity in taste. Consumers will no longer accept only black cars; they want a much wider range of choice. Companies are therefore having to cater to a much greater diversity in the market. Mass production systems which can only produce a narrow product range will no longer do. Second, flexible systems use much more sophisticated technology than was possible even thirty years ago. This increase in sophistication, of course, comes largely from a much greater use of smaller and more powerful computers. An important consequence is that machines displace human labour. For example, what now appears a simple technology, electronic point-of-sale equipment, means that supermarket checkouts can be faster and use fewer staff. Since the sale of items is electronically recorded, stock control is much easier, again resulting in the employment of fewer staff. In manufacturing, computer-controlled equipment can be programmed to perform different tasks and turn out different products, making it possible to produce goods cost-effectively in small batches. It is no longer necessary, in other words, to have machines on production lines dedicated to the production of only one item. Technology has become more flexible.

A third feature of flexible systems is that, while management in Fordist arrangements tended to be centralized, in more flexible firms it is more likely to rely on looser and more decentralized methods. Workers are expected to work in teams, which have targets to meet but which take responsibility for meeting them. The system of control does not rely, therefore, on direct and continuing instruction, but on the setting of a framework within which workers are given responsibility. Fourth, flexible systems have an effect on the jobs that workers do. Whereas in more bureaucratic systems they become specialized at one task, flexibility means some movement between different tasks, a movement that demands a wider range of skills. If firms have to make flexible responses to rapid changes in their markets, they will have to be able freely to vary the number of staff that they employ. Bureaucratic systems may mean predictable employment for a considerable period of time. Flexible systems imply unpredictable employment with periods of unemployment. In order to cope with changing the number of people employed and changing the kind of work that they do, firms will think of their workforce as composed of a small and highly skilled core of more or less permanently employed workers and a peripheral group of workers who will be temporary, part-time, or employed by subcontractors or agents, and who can be brought in when necessary.

It is unwise to overstate the differences between the two ways of organizing production systems and the inevitability of the transition between them. Bureaucratic ways of organizing work clearly persist in large companies and public bodies; there is not much evidence of an increase in multi-skilling as a result of more flexible arrangements; subcontracting has been used for a long time as a way of managing labour in fluctuating markets; and Fordist, bureaucratic methods are actually flexible in the sense that comparatively unskilled workers are relatively easy to lay off when markets turn down.

Despite reservations of this kind, the distinction between Fordist and flexible methods still has validity. But what does flexibility mean for everyday work lives? Has work become more or less of a curse? The public answers given to these questions in newspapers or on television and by politicians often seem contradictory. On the one hand, flexibility is said to have benefits for workers. It offers, it is claimed, the opportunity for part-time work for those who want it, especially women; people are more able to work from home; flexible working hours may suit some people; there is the possibility of more skilled and varied work, perhaps by assembling a portfolio of different types of work for different employers; and management is less intrusive, with workers taking responsibility for their own jobs. On the other hand, it is also said that job insecurity has increased; hours of work are lengthening or are inconveniently arranged; more is demanded of employees, leading to increased stress; and workers move house more often to answer the demands of their work, breaking the ties of wider family and friends.

On the face of it, the evidence would seem to support the pessimists. As I noted earlier in the chapter, in the larger European countries, the rate of unemployment has risen since the early 1970s. Unemployment is only one index of job insecurity that might be created by more flexible organizations. The number of jobs that an individual has in a lifetime is another. A tendency for flexible firms to lay off workers in response to changing market conditions might well produce greater job mobility among employees. One study[16] compared groups starting work at different times since 1951. Those groups entering the labour market in later years tended to leave jobs more frequently than those starting earlier, implying a decline in the length of time in each job. The major cause of this is the likelihood of being laid off.[17] These uncertainties in the labour market are further demonstrated by the work destinations of those leaving full-time education. In the 1950s, the great majority of these went into full-time jobs. Now, an increasing proportion go into part-time or self-employed jobs, and fully one-third are unemployed. The young also change their jobs more often than their elders did when they started out in work.

One of the more dramatic changes in employment since the 1950s has been the growth in part-time employment, which is largely taken up by women. For women, part-time work is a permanent state, while men tend to go in and out of it. In the 1980s, for instance, of an increase in the number of jobs of all kinds of about 1 million, fully 930,000 were part-time and only 33,000 were full-time. Generally, those on part-time contracts, who tend to have less job security, fit in better with flexible working methods. So also do employees who work flexible hours, in the evenings and at weekends. Eighteen per cent of men and 25 per cent of women, mostly in clerical occupations, now work in this way, a very significant rise over the position even twenty years ago.

As firms look for more flexible methods, one would expect them to subcontract more of their work. As the market waxes and wanes, it is the subcontractor that absorbs the fluctuation. And, indeed, there has been a rise in self-employment, particularly in the 1980s and 1990s. In addition, there is a disproportionate growth in employment in small companies that are likely to be the recipients of subcontracted work. One way in which people are self-employed is by working at home. In fact, a very small number of people do this (about 3 per cent of the employed population, though there are indications that this figure could be rising). However, an analysis of this type of work shows that many homeworkers are really like part-time or full-time workers who just work at home, often under conditions far from ideal. The glamorous image of home-working given to us may be of computers and technology. The reality is childminding, ironing, sewing and stuffing envelopes.[18]

Earlier in the chapter, I showed that, although hours of work have steadily decreased in the last one hundred years, more recently they have levelled off. There is no evidence, in other words, that there is any more stress on workers arising from longer hours of work, even if those hours are becoming more inconveniently arranged. However, work might have become more of a curse because workers are forced to work harder, to pack more in. Perhaps work has become *intensified*. Such intensification could arise from a number of changes. For example, one of the principles of the flexible firm is a management structure which emphasizes team-working and the delegation of responsibility to the team. In such an arrangement, people do not necessarily have fixed job descriptions or occupational titles that go with fixed salaries. Instead, they have particular skills that they bring to a variety of projects, and they move from task to task. Team-working is considerably more common than it was and, furthermore, almost a quarter of employees in the private sector have some element of their pay dependent on the performance of their team, a proportion that has risen from 6 per cent ten years ago.[19] Interestingly, an increasing proportion of the working population say that the pressure at work comes from colleagues and not directly from management.

The evidence from a number of studies is that there has been greater intensification of work.[20] If people are asked to compare the effort that they put into their job now compared with that expended five or ten years previously, the majority clearly believe that they work harder. A question like that is potentially unreliable, since it asks people to look back at the past, and our memories of the past are often influenced by our feelings about the present. However, these conclusions about the intensity of work are confirmed by other surveys that ask the same questions about effort at work in successive years. The amount of work effort put in *beyond* what is required and the amount actually demanded by the employer have increased.

Does flexibility and intensification of the kind revealed in these data result in greater stress, loss of a sense of well-being and reduced work satisfaction, as is often claimed? A recent study[21] has concluded that employees' satisfaction with their jobs has declined in every respect since a comparable study was conducted in 1992, whether it concerns pay, the nature or variety of the work, the availability of training, or job prospects. However, the respect in which employees express most dissatisfaction is in the number of hours worked and in the intensity of that work. That dissatisfaction is especially pronounced at both ends of the occupational hierarchy – professionals and unskilled workers. Those with university degrees also express greater dissatisfaction with their hours worked than those with fewer educational qualifications. This seems a paradoxical conclusion in certain respects. At the start of this chapter, I showed how, over a fairly long period, the hours worked by employees have declined steadily. However, this really refers to the official working week. If one includes paid and *unpaid* overtime, indications are that the total number of hours worked began to increase at the close of the twentieth century.[22] When asked why they worked long hours, those in managerial or supervisory occupations tended to point to the requirements of the job, or the need to meet deadlines, and it is these people who will be putting in unpaid overtime. Other employees cited the possibility of earning more money.[23]

It is commonly believed that longer working hours and a greater intensity of work will lead to greater stress at work. The newspapers are full of stories about the levels of compensation awarded to employees who have been stressed at work and whose health has broken down as a result. New conditions have appeared that are apparently caused by work practices, such as repetitive strain injury. Work stress has been estimated to lose 5 to 6 million work days per year in the UK as people are absent from work with a bewildering variety of symptoms. And, as a recent study found, the experience of stress is an important component of the way that people talk about their work. Here is one respondent from this study talking about being a steward on a cross-channel ferry:

> It's constant pressure all the time. You've got to perform to a certain level, no matter how tired you are, how many nasty horrible people you get. You have got to have that front on all the time, and it is very hard to smile at somebody when they are shouting at you or while being awkward; or just downright arseholes.[24]

But, as the authors of the study point out, the pathway from the characteristics of work, whether those are longer hours, flexible work patterns, or greater intensity of work, to the symptoms of stress, as physical or mental illness, is complex. There may well be greater stress at work produced in the ways described above, but it may not be so clear that they lead in a simple way to the *experience* of stress. After all, work was almost certainly harder and more pressured in the first half of the twentieth century, and even more so during the industrial revolution in the first half of the nineteenth. Those periods did not appear to be accompanied, however, by the symptoms of stress that are so common in modern times. Maybe it is the case, therefore, that work has not got harder but that workers have become less resilient.

If that conclusion were true, however, how would one explain the epidemic of stress, especially as work *does* seem to have got more pressured over the last twenty or thirty years and one cannot dismiss the symptoms of stress as *mere* imagination? One possibility considered by the authors is that making claims about stress is one of the few ways open to workers of blocking the pressures that employers apply. Since the 1980s the power of trade unions and of collective bargaining has declined. Arguing that the intensification of work is leading to employee stress can, especially given the efficacy of health and safety legislation, help to moderate the pressures of work. However, an additional and more powerful factor is the way that people think and talk about work, stress and illness.

The argument is that work has got harder but workers have also become less resilient. The way that contemporary culture works makes us all *interpret* our feelings about work pressures as stress which issues in illness. Firstly, we have all come to feel that we are very vulnerable. There are countless health scares which make daily life seem very dangerous. We are told that much of what we eat will make us ill rather than nourish us. Microwave cookers, televisions, mobile phones, and power cables project unseen waves which will harm us. It even matters which way round a baby is laid in a cot. Secondly, a tradition of British stoicism and resilience has been replaced by an emphasis on the open demonstration of emotional suffering. There is a tendency to claim the status of victim in order to obtain the support of others, a tendency equally common for figures in the public eye – Princess Diana, for example – as it is for ordinary people in everyday life. A consequence is the encouragement of passivity. Thirdly, more and more states of mind or body are thought of as illnesses in need of treatment. More and more new conditions appear and more and more therapists are recruited to handle them. Work stress is no longer opposed by collective or political action but is instead translated into illness states which require therapeutic intervention.

This is a challenging argument and it needs to be clear what is being said. It is argued that a society's culture, the way in which people think about themselves, is more likely to make people ill than the pressures of work. This is not to say that work has not got harder. More importantly, it is not the case that people do not manifest real and serious symptoms of individualized illness which they attribute to stress.

So, is work a curse? Much of the evidence offered in this chapter would suggest that it is and that it is getting worse. For example, work is becoming more intense and is giving less satisfaction. Hours of work can be at unsociable times and, for some, they are becoming longer. There has been a marked rise in the proportion of households without work. On the other hand, we have to understand the motives that impel people to work. It is tempting, particularly if one believes that work is a curse, to say that people work for the money and that is all there is to it. Actually, the position is more complex, and work is central to people's lives for a variety of reasons. Work is more interesting and involving than staying at home. In an American study,[25] Arlie Hochschild found that both men and women preferred to go to work and escape the tedium of housework. Employment gives identity and purpose, rewarding relationships with fellow workers – and it structures the day. A study of skilled shipyard workers in Britain shows the way in which money is not the only reward of employment. In answer to the question 'Why do you work?', two of these workers replied:

> For self-respect – I don't want to become a social parasite. And I don't want to be bored. It's good for meeting people and I get a lot of job satisfaction, and for the money too.

> Making a living and getting the self-respect of doing something productive. It gives me peace of mind.[26]

And this applies to all kinds of work. From another study, here are two women factory workers speaking of their work:

> It's changed my life going out to work. I couldn't bear to stay in the house and not to work . . . I used to be very quiet. Coming out to work has changed me.

> After a couple of weeks on the sick, you want to go back to work. You get bored, you get lazy . . . You need something to get up for in the morning.[27]

Work, in other words, is contradictory. The pessimistic and the optimistic views of modern work could both be true. Even the changes in patterns of work may have this ambivalent character. Employees *may* be offered greater freedom to go part-time, to work from home, or to choose when to work. Team-working *may* give greater satisfaction and job control. But there is a price to be paid for these freedoms. And the real point is that some people may be able to benefit from the opportunities offered by flexibility, while others will simply suffer from the insecurity and stress. Those with highly marketable skills, in information technology or financial management, for instance, can benefit from flexibility. Those without will not. This inequality is the topic of the next chapter.

# 6

# Does inequality matter?

Work is of two kinds: first, altering the position of matter at or near the earth's surface relatively to other such matter; second, telling other people to do so. The first kind is unpleasant and ill paid; the second is pleasant and highly paid.

Bertrand Russell

Many parents pay their children for doing routine domestic tasks. Apparently, boys are paid on average five times as much as girls for emptying the dishwasher.[1] In the 1990s in England and Wales, if you had a working-class occupation, you were almost three times more likely to die between the ages of twenty and sixty-four than someone with a professional occupation.[2] Afro-Caribbean people in Britain are almost twice as likely to suffer from burglary as white people.[3] All these are contemporary examples of inequality between people.

Of course, people can be different – and unequal – in lots of different ways. Our neighbours and friends come in different sizes, are of very different physical attractiveness and have different amounts of money. Some are happy, some are not. Some are plagued by illness while others seem to be bounding with health into old age. Some just seem to be lucky. Difference and inequality are, of course, not the same thing. Furthermore, there are tensions between the ideals of equality and diversity. Societies which seek to reduce the dangers of inequality may do so at the cost of suppressing some of the differences between people. And policies designed to increase the tolerance of diversity, encouraging the emergence of different kinds of schools, for example, may have the effect of widening inequalities.

Our everyday lives will be full of observation of differences and inequalities. However, we have to be wary of the commonsense of everyday here, since the *patterning* of these inequalities may not always be obvious. I mean three things by this. First, the various ways in which people are unequal may be closely related to one another. For example, the possession of financial resources, physical size and the likelihood of escaping depression and ill health tend to be associated with each other. In a more indirect way, even beauty is connected with wealth. This is not only because some people have the money to look good. It is also because the idea of beauty – what counts as good looks – may be determined by those who have wealth and prestige. For example, the eighteenth-century ideal of feminine beauty was a very pale complexion, and white lead was used as make-up. This was the ideal favoured by the aristocracy, who wished to distinguish themselves from those who had to work for a living and hence had skins browned by the sun and weather. More recently, those who are about to undergo plastic surgery to improve their looks may show to the surgeon a picture of a celebrity that they wish to resemble. Second, inequalities may be literally invisible. It is an underlying argument of this book that everyday life tends to be lived largely within a particular social circle. Typically, we associate with others like ourselves and not with those more or less fortunate. There is a considerable degree of social segregation whereby work lives and leisure pursuits are undertaken together with people like us, a homogeneity reinforced by the way that residential districts house people of very similar background. It is partly this lack of experience of inequality that can give a particular view of the world and lead people to say, for example, that there is no poverty in Britain or that single mothers have plenty of money. Third, and most important, everyday talk about difference and inequality tends to be about *individuals*. Actually, the most interesting and significant social and sociological point about inequality is that it is generalized across individuals. Society is structured into social groups in which inequalities of many kinds are concentrated. Sociologists typically use a geological analogy here and speak of societies as *stratified*, as composed of social groups arranged in a hierarchy. The way in which societies involve such stratification systems is concealed from our everyday lives by the fact that we interact with individuals, not social groups, and that those individuals share so many characteristics with us. Even if unrecognized, however, these structures of inequality will have profound effects on everyday life. This chapter, then, is about the *patterning* of inequality.

The question of this chapter is whether this patterned inequality matters. In answering the question, I need to make a distinction between inequality of condition and inequality of opportunity. Many of the examples that I have given so far are inequalities of condition. Thus, it might well matter whether some people are poorer, run a greater risk of ill health or have worse housing than others. But this is a different issue from whether some have different opportunities in life. For example, a society may be thought unjust if some of those who have ability are unable to obtain the educational opportunities to make use of that ability.

## Inequality of condition

Inequality can arise from different sources – ethnicity, gender or occupation, for example – and be manifested in various ways. Thus, most ethnic groups suffer more chronic illness than the comparable white population, are poorer, and tend to be tenants rather than owner-occupiers. For example, those of Bangladeshi origin have a rate of unemployment three times that of whites.[4] Or, for gender, in the late 1990s women earned 81 per cent of a man's hourly wage for the same type of work.[5] However, the most important source of inequality is occupation, which has a greater impact on chances in life than other factors. Indeed, much of the inequality related to ethnicity or gender derives from their relationship to occupation. It is the fact that women or ethnic minorities go into relatively poorly paid occupations, by comparison with men or the white population, that largely explains their unequal position in society.

In turn, occupation is significant because it is the major determinant of income and wealth. Of course, inequality can be manifested in other ways – as variations in power or prestige, for instance. However, as a rule, money, power and prestige go together. Thus the upper classes in Britain have money that derives from highly paid occupations, inheritance, or participation in successful businesses. They have power that derives from their positions in organizations, from political position or from knowing people who are in those positions. They have prestige in that their doings are the subject of gossip or, occasionally, veneration. That prestige can be turned into money, as appearances in *Hello* or *OK* can testify.

The starting point for the analysis of inequality, therefore, is the way that income and wealth are distributed. An individual's or household's income consists of money received from employment, occupational pensions, investments, social security benefits and state pensions. In the United Kingdom, in the 1990s, the richest one-tenth of households received almost nine times as much income before tax as the poorest one-tenth.[6] We tend to assume that the effect of taxes will be to reduce inequalities of this kind. In fact, the opposite is the case. After direct and indirect taxes, the richest one-tenth of households had more than eleven times the income of the poorest one-tenth. This paradoxical result arises out of the different effects of direct and indirect taxation. The former, income tax, for example, does affect higher-earning households dispro-portionately. The latter, such as VAT, however, affects lower-earning households more, because so much of their total expenditure is effec-tively subject to tax. It is important to note too that the households at the top and the bottom of the income distribution are not all of the same type. The poorest one-tenth of households, for example, contain twice the proportion of families with children as the richest one-tenth. This is partly due to inequalities as people grow older. Household income rises sharply for married couples before they have children, falls while they have young children, and rises again to its peak when the children are between sixteen and twenty-four. From that peak, income falls steeply towards retirement.

How has this pattern of income inequality changed over time? In the period 1949 to the middle of the 1970s, the distribution of income after tax appeared to be fairly stable. There was a small degree of equaliza-tion in the mid-1960s to the early 1970s, and by the mid-1970s the share of post-tax income taken by the bottom one-fifth of individuals was at its highest since the war. However, since the late 1970s the distribution of income has widened again, with the 1980s showing a very rapid growth in income inequality. Between 1978 and 1993, the share of income taken by the bottom one-fifth of households fell from 10 per cent to 8 per cent, while the richest one-fifth increased their share from 35 per cent to 42 per cent. In the 1990s the distribution remained roughly stable. Income inequality did not increase yet further, but it has also not decreased during the period in office of a Labour government. Britain is one of the most unequal societies in Europe. For example, the country records the second highest proportion of people among twelve European countries living in poverty (defined as those living in households with incomes below half the national average). It is important to realize that this does not tell us anything about the fate of individual households over time. Actually, individual household incomes will fluctuate from year to year. However, they do not fluctuate very far. This point is prob-ably most important for those at the bottom of the income distribution, for it suggests that people may move in and out of poverty over time.[7] I return to this later in the chapter.

There is no single cause of the growth in inequality during the 1980s. Undoubtedly, taxation and benefits policies begun under the Thatcher governments, and continued since, have had an effect. So also has a rising rate of unemployment, a collapse in trade union power and national bargaining structures, and a relative increase in rates of pay to the better-off. An additional important cause is the relationship between work, individuals and households. The number of households without a working member rose sharply in the early 1980s but, when economic recovery came, employment was disproportionately concentrated in households whose members already had work. Britain is increasingly a society of work-rich and work-poor households.[8]

In considering inequality, wealth – the total stock of assets which could in principle be sold – is in many ways more important than income. These assets can yield income which is likely to be more secure than wages and salaries from employment, and that power can be transferred to others. In the 1920s the richest 1 per cent of the population owned fully 60 per cent of the wealth in England and Wales. The poorest 90 per cent owned only 11 per cent. Throughout the century until the 1970s, this gap narrowed considerably until, in 1971, the top 1 per cent owned 29 per cent, a little less than the bottom 10 per cent. This process had stopped, however, by the 1980s. Thus, half of the wealth in the country was owned by the richest 10 per cent in the mid-1970s, a figure almost unchanged in the early 1990s. Any redistribution that has taken place has not benefited the poorest people but has taken the form of a relative increase in the wealth of the rich at the expense of the very rich. In sum, wealth remains very concentrated in the hands of a few and is more unequally distributed than income.[9]

Poverty is one of the more obvious consequences of an unequal dis-tribution of income and wealth. A commonly used measure is the pro-portion of households whose income falls below half of the average income of all households in the country. By this measure, 24 per cent of the population in the UK were in poverty in the mid-1990s. Strikingly, the proportion in poverty has grown considerably in recent years. In the late 1970s, for instance, only 9 per cent of the population lived in house-holds with less than half of the average income. Another way of putting the same point is to note that, up to the late 1970s, there was a gradual tendency to share out the benefits of economic growth more equally. From the late 1970s until the mid-1990s, however, rising national pros-perity went disproportionately to the already rich. Within the last ten years or so, the proportion of those in poverty has fallen back a little. Particularly likely to be living in poverty are those in part-time work, the unemployed, single parents, pensioners and the long-term sick. It is notable that about a quarter of those living in poverty are working but earn too little and, of the remainder, the majority are children, those over sixty-five or the ill. This hardly confirms the picture of the poor as able-bodied scroungers. Especially striking are the numbers of children who are members of households in poverty. In the UK in the mid-1990s, more than one-quarter of all children lived in poverty.

The UK has a higher proportion of people in poverty than most comparable Western countries. For example, in 1994 Britain had the second highest rate of all European Union countries. Of course, in an absolute sense, the poor in the UK are better off than much of the population of, say, southern Africa. Nonetheless, however often one hears comparisons of this sort, one still cannot deny that poverty in the UK is an affront to the country's own standards of a civilized society – especially in one of the most prosperous countries in the world.

The boundary separating the poor is not only a moveable one, it is also permeable. In other words, people move in and out of poverty. Thus, of those who are poor in any one year, almost half are out of poverty by the next year. However, those who are no longer poor are at risk of dropping back into poverty in the future. One study shows that one-third of individuals have experienced poverty in at least one year in six.[10] It is important not to exaggerate the significance of this mobility, for people may move in and out of poverty, but they do not move very far in income terms.

This mobility makes it very difficult, therefore, to see the poor as constituting an underclass of people permanently locked into that position. And a substantial number of people will have experienced the deprivations of poverty and the relentless daily struggle to get by on a small income. One study found that one in five adults and one in ten children had gone without food in the previous month because they could not afford it.[11] Water, electricity and gas are likely to be cut off. Healthy eating becomes difficult. An interviewee in one study said of her husband, who had a stomach ulcer:

> The doctor told him he needs fish and chicken regularly but we can't afford it . . . We seem to live off chips and potatoes . . . He should have low-fat meat every day . . . We only have a cooked meal three times a week to cut down on gas.[12]

Material deprivation of this kind is not the only consequence of poverty. Poor people do not *want* to be in that state and frequently feel ashamed.

> I have actually had to swallow my pride 'till it hurts . . . It makes me feel like a complete failure because I had such high ideals . . . I wanted to give my children the best, not to the point of spoiling them, but just so they could, you know, have confidence in themselves. So when I can't do that it makes me feel I'm failing.[13]

There is also a connection with health in that there is a long-standing but simple relationship between income and the risk of premature death. Every step down the class ladder, for both men and women, brings a greater chance of early death. A gradient of this kind exists for most of the major causes of death. For example, the death rates for coronary heart disease are about 40 per cent higher for manual workers than they are for non-manual workers. Furthermore, these inequalities are increasing. For example, although life expectancy is increasing for everybody, the richer benefit more than the poorer. Between 1972 and 1996, life expectancy for men at the top of the income gradient increased by almost six years, but for men in the lowest social class the increase was less than two years. In the 1970s, death rates were twice as high among unskilled manual workers as among professionals. And it has not improved. In the 1990s the death rate is three times higher.[14]

The mechanisms that connect income or social class position with health and ill health are complex. Material circumstances play a role in that the quality of housing and environment and the living standards that money can buy all have a clear relationship to health. Also relevant are behavioural characteristics such as a tendency to smoke or to avoid exercise, which are related to both class and health. More psychological factors have also been shown to have a part. For example, if people perceive themselves to be relatively deprived in comparison to others, they are more prone to illness and recover less quickly. In many ways, the proposition that ill health is related to income is not altogether surprising. What is surprising, however, is the finding that the health of a whole society is dependent on its degree of inequality rather than on how wealthy it is. For instance, the United States is undoubtedly a more wealthy society than Greece, and is a more unequal one, yet the expectation of life in Greece is higher than that in the United States.[15]

In the language of contemporary public debate, especially since the election of a Labour government in 1997, these consequences of inequality are aspects of social exclusion. Those at the bottom have such a high level of absolute deprivation that they are excluded from social participation to all intents and purposes. They suffer illness and disease, poor food, lack of meaningful work, limited access to education, very much reduced social networks and poverty. *And* they feel bad about it and are more likely to blame themselves than anyone else, as the quotations reproduced above indicate. This condensation of deprivation can be expressed in the language of citizenship. It is as if the poor are not fully citizens; they cannot participate in society. Such a conception of social exclusion leads to social policies of a particular kind – attempts to raise educational attainment, health promotion schemes, welfare systems designed to target the particularly vulnerable. This, however, is treating social inequality simply as producing undesirable consequences for a relatively small group – the socially excluded. Now, I have already shown that this group is not so small. Even in only six years, fully one-third of the population has been touched by poverty.

Inequalities that are too great matter, because no civilized society should tolerate a situation in which many of its citizens are so extensively deprived. It might be argued, however, that such inequalities are *fair* because they reflect the distribution of talent and ability in the population. There may be inequality of condition but perhaps there is also equality of opportunity. In order to explore this idea I need to introduce the idea of systems of inequality, especially of social class.

## Systems of inequality

So far I have presented the issue of inequality as if it were a smooth gradient from the richest to the poorest, rather like the way in which one might arrange a school class of children from the tallest to the shortest. Now, while it is useful to present inequality in this way, it is very important to realize that power, prestige and money are organized together to form *systems* of inequality. These systems take the form of stratification, a division of the population into layers.

Systems of inequality – or stratification – will differ from society to society and, historically, several types of system can be distinguished. *Slavery* has been found in societies as diverse as classical Athens and eighteenth-century America. The crucial feature of such societies is that slaves are owned by their masters. Such ownership might arise by purchase or by capture in war. Although we may tend to think of slaves as working at the most menial and exhausting occupations, as in the plantations of the Caribbean or what is now the United States or the mines of South America, slaves in ancient societies could occupy quite senior positions as administrators. However, whatever their role, the lives of slaves were clearly limited by the fact that they were owned. Some were freed by their masters or escaped but, generally, slave societies were very rigid. It is possible to argue that the modern world has the remnants of slavery in the use of forced labour in some societies.

Systems of stratification based on *caste* are typically found in the Indian sub-continent. Position in the caste system is based on birth, and it is therefore not possible to change one's caste. The relationships between castes are expressed in terms of honour or prestige, supported by codes of behaviour and by the Hindu religion. In particular, there are strong taboos that prevent mixing between the castes.[16] One caste is named the untouchables because its members literally cannot be touched by castes above them in the hierarchy. Caste-like systems have been found elsewhere in the world. This is particularly true where racial or ethnic distinctions are involved. For example, in the southern states of the United States or in South Africa until recently, blacks and whites were segregated from each other by legal measures, by custom, or by taboos such as disgust at intermarriage.

*Estates* occurred in feudal Europe and in China and Japan. The aristocracy comprised the first estate and was headed by the king or emperor. The second estate was made up of the clergy in Europe and the samurai in Japan. Commoners constituted the third estate, and in Japan there was a fourth estate of outcasts. The system worked as a series of rights and duties owed by estates to each other. In feudal Europe, it was to some extent also supported by religious beliefs which asserted the divine right of kings. A remnant of the estates system persists in Britain in the prestige that continues to be given to the monarchy and the aristocracy and the deference that is shown to titles of all kinds.

Traces of slavery and of the estates characteristic of aristocratic societies persist in modern times. Caste continues to inform daily life in India, but its significance is waning under the impact of economic changes and attempts to legislate against it. The contemporary world is, however, dominated by a fourth kind of stratification system – *social class*.

All stratification systems are founded in the interrelationships between money, power and prestige. Higher strata have more of all these attributes, although, in different systems, different elements have relatively more importance. Prestige and honour are particularly significant in caste systems, power in slavery. In addition, all systems of stratification have, in effect, to regulate the relationships between strata. Caste, slavery and estate systems are underpinned by law, force and religion. Social contact, especially marriage, is prevented by custom and taboo and position is determined by birth. The result is that these systems are fairly rigid and do not allow much, if any, mobility from one stratum to another. Systems based on social class, on the other hand, do not erect such firm barriers between strata. They depend, furthermore, on economic differences between groups of individuals.

## Social class

Social class, largely determined by occupation, is a very important source of social division in contemporary societies. Its significance does not lie solely in differences in command over economic resources. People in the same class share tastes in everything from food to music, have similar consumption patterns, have children who are likely to have similar paths through life, live in much the same kind of place, and will have a life expectancy different from those in other classes. Class condenses and organizes the experience of life. As we shall see, this does not mean to say that all people within a social class are the same, or that no person can move from one class to another, or that the boundaries between social classes are perfectly clear, or, indeed, that sociologists are sure how many social classes there are.

The conventional position is that there are three broad social classes in Britain – the upper class, middle class and working class. The upper class is very small, composed of between 1 per cent and 3 per cent of the population, and is made up of the independently wealthy, those who own or control productive resources, and senior managers in large enterprises.[17] I have already shown how wealthy the top 1 per cent of the population is and how recently they have maintained that privileged position. It would be a great mistake, however, to think of this wealth as passively enjoyed. The upper class *uses* its wealth and position. Its members occupy strategic positions of influence in companies, and one might describe the core of the class as being those who have substantial business interests which overlap and interlock. It is important to note, however, that this business core is closely connected with other members of the upper class at the top of other fields such as politics, the civil service, the judiciary and the professions. In addition, members of the upper class form very effective networks of other kinds. There is substantial intermarriage, which gives the class a certain unity based on kinship and marriage. These connections are further extended by the ties of friendship and acquaintance, which are often summarized in the phrase 'old boy' network' and which allow a smooth connection between social and business activities. Contacts of this kind are possible partly because of common background. Members of the upper classes associate together easily, because they have the same tastes, attitudes and inclinations, formed by similarity of family background, school and university. The result is that the upper class is enclosed and self-recruiting. Current members of the upper class are likely to be the offspring of wealthy individuals, and their sons and daughters, similarly, are likely to occupy upper-class positions. The coherence, wealth and power of the upper class are reflected in its prestige. To some extent an upper-class lifestyle is still celebrated and presented as desirable in newspapers and magazines. Despite this, however, upper-class people probably display their lives less conspicuously than they used to do; in this sense the class is becoming less visible.

The middle class is formed by three broad sections – small businessmen and women, those in professional and management occupations, and white-collar workers.[18] It grew dramatically in the twentieth century as manual work declined, and particular occupations within the middle class increased disproportionately over the century. For example, the higher professions have increased fivefold, managers by four times, and those in clerical occupations between threefold and fourfold. There are also gender differences in these movements. Both men and women have shifted out of manual into non-manual work, but men have tended to go into the higher white-collar jobs as managers and professionals, while women have disproportionately entered the more routine and poorly paid white-collar occupations.

One result of the growth in these occupations is that employers in small businesses, including shopkeepers, small traders and manufacturers, who constituted an important sector of the middle class in the nineteenth century, have become much less significant. Their numbers have steadily declined until recently, when the proportion of the workforce that is self-employed rose slightly from just under 7 per cent in the early 1980s to over 10 per cent in the 1990s. People in these occupations are in an ambiguous position. On the one hand, they have considerable control over their own work situation. On the other, many of them have earnings that are little more than those of routine white-collar workers or even manual workers.

People in professional and management occupations have employment advantages so different from other white-collar workers that they are sometimes referred to as a separate class – the service class. This is a group that has grown very rapidly. It has doubled in size since the end of the Second World War and now constitutes about 30 per cent of the population. They are paid much better, usually have a clear career path through which they are promoted, and have better associated benefits such as occupational pensions. Their work is, as a rule, varied and interesting. Perhaps most important of all, they have a substantial amount of control over their own work – and a corresponding degree of responsibility. At one time these were also relatively secure jobs. However, as firms have become ever more cost-conscious, they have tried to take out layers of management, and it is no longer the case that professional qualifications or a management role guarantee jobs for life.

A large part of the middle class does not have these advantages. People working as clerks, secretaries or telesales assistants have jobs that consist of fairly routine tasks, attracting little prestige, which are often highly mechanized. They are relatively poorly paid and have little control over what they do or how they do it. It is difficult to talk of a career in connection with much white-collar work. These jobs, in other words, are not greatly dissimilar from working-class ones. Over the twentieth century, the gap in earnings between non-manual and manual occupations narrowed considerably and there is now little difference between the more routine white-collar occupations and the more skilled manual ones. On the other hand, despite the narrowing, there is a continuing gap between this section of the middle class and those in working-class occupations. Manual workers tend to work longer hours for their wages, their earnings tend to decrease as they near retirement, and they are more prone to unemployment. As much as anything, however, the difference between the social classes is a question of culture. Those who are in white-collar occupations, however routine or poorly paid, do not think of themselves as working class. Although at the turn of the twentieth century clerical jobs were largely taken by men, now they attract four times as many women as men. For many young women thinking about taking their first job, office work is greatly more attractive than jobs in a factory or shop.

Within the last fifty years, working-class occupations have undergone considerable change. As the last chapter showed, service industries are replacing manufacturing or extractive industries as sources of employment in the United Kingdom. Working-class jobs in the mines, in steelworks or in large-scale manufacturing are being replaced by ones in hotels, the leisure industries or supermarkets, new jobs which typically involve employment in smaller enterprises that are not heavily unionized. Again, as the last chapter showed, the working-class jobs that have been created tend to be taken increasingly by women and are more likely to be part-time and demand flexible working patterns.

Many of the jobs created in the growing service sector are manual working-class jobs, but there are disproportionately larger numbers of white-collar jobs. As a result, the working class has shrunk as the middle class has grown. One rough index of this is the decline in the numbers of manual workers. In 1951, some 70 per cent of the workforce were manual workers. Forty years later that proportion had dropped to about 40 per cent.[19]

Like the middle class, the working class is diverse. It is comprised of workers in occupations that demand a great deal of skill and training and those that require very little. Fifty years ago or so, the highly trained members of the working class were those with craft skills – engineers, for example – who had periods of apprenticeship. Now they are more likely to be technicians who have formal educational qualifications. At the other extreme, a great many of the new manual jobs in the service sector require very little skill. There is a similar diversity in pay and conditions of work. Although the newer jobs are poorly paid and insecure, there still are relatively well-paid and secure jobs in the engineering and chemical industries.

These diversities have prompted many to say that there is a growing rift within the working class. On the one hand, there are working-class households in which husband and wife are both permanently employed in occupations which give them a good standard of living. On the other, there are households whose members are unable to secure permanent employment and, when they do, have to take jobs with poor pay and irregular hours. The latter group is sometimes referred to as an underclass in which is concentrated poverty and low educational achievement. The idea that there are two sections of the working class – the rough and the respectable – has been with us at least since Victorian times and today it is repeated in newspaper accounts of crime on sink estates, delinquent behaviour in schools, single parenting and dependence on welfare payments, and the black economy. While, as we shall see later, it is true that there is greater inequality in the UK, leading to social exclusion for a substantial proportion of the population, it is less clear that there is a distinctive underclass. Certainly, the position is not very like that in the United States, where there appears to be an underclass differentiated by ethnicity as well as poverty.

In describing the class structure, so far I have concentrated on features such as pay and the capacity to control one's work. How then do people identify *themselves* as members of classes? Opinion polls have found that a substantial majority of those questioned (over two-thirds) believe that Britain is a class-ridden society.[20] Furthermore, in a systematic study of social class conducted in the late 1980s, over 90 per cent of the respondents felt able to place themselves in a particular social class.[21] A placing in a class usually involves rejecting membership of another class. The point is illustrated by a study of the way in which working-class women experience social class. The study followed for twelve years a group of young women training as care assistants.[22] Its conclusion was that, although the women did not use the term class, they were all too conscious of the categorization. In particular, they wanted *not* to identify with the working class or, rather, with their view of it. For them, working class means:

> They're rough. You can always tell. Rough, you know, the women are as common as muck, you know, always have a fag in their mouths, the men are dead rough, you know.[23]

The group aspired to a way of life that would differentiate them from the rough working class. They tried to dress or to decorate their houses in a way they thought of as middle class. But, at the same time, they felt insecure and anxious about these attempts, as if they might be found out. As one said:

All the time you've got to weigh everything up: is it too tarty? Will I look like a right slag in it? What will people think? It drives me mad that every time you go to put your clothes on you have to think 'do I look dead common? Is it rough? Do I look like a dog?'[24]

Their occupation and background have driven them in one way but their aspirations have driven them in another.

Inequality in modern Britain is largely organized as social class. It should be clear from what I have said that this is not to say that social classes are solid lumps, internally consistent and wholly distinguishable from one another. Quite the contrary: they are composed of fractions that are very different from one another, and the boundaries cannot be established with certainty. For some purposes one may want to redraw the class map a little. For example, in the next section, I will want to treat what I have described as the service class and the upper class as one class.[25] Nonetheless, social classes are important social entities. The question that I now want to answer is: is inequality of the social class system fair?

## Inequality of opportunity

Even if a society is unequal, even if there are substantial differences in income, health or housing standards between social classes, perhaps that society is still a fair or just one. It may well be, in other words, that there is equality of opportunity. That is, people of similar abilities have similar chances of reaching occupations that will pay them well whatever their class of origin. This is the view that, unequal as they may be, modern societies are meritocratic, positions in the occupational structure being filled on the basis of ability and talent.

There is another kind of argument that comes to much the same conclusion. So, it is often suggested that, for the common good of society, it is important to ensure that the most competent persons occupy the most important positions. To do that they will have to be given incentives, which will mean that they are paid more than others. Inequality is simply the outcome of the need to incentivize. Very frequently in the newspapers one reads of pay awards to chief executives using precisely this argument.

To put it more systematically, the argument might run something like this.[26] Certain positions in society are of critical importance to the society at large and require high degrees of skill and experience in those who fill them. There will be relatively few individuals in any society who have the talent to be successful in these positions. The development of talent into the necessary skill and experience demands training, application and hard work. To induce talented individuals to come forward, undergo a period of training *and* perform well in the job requires a system of differential reward. Without such differences in reward, talented individuals would have no incentive to exert themselves.

These two arguments about the inevitability or the justice of inequality are often countered in the same way. The counter-argument is simply that those who occupy privileged positions have the power to defend them, thereby making the degree of inequality more extreme than would be justified by the need for incentive. The rich will therefore take steps to avoid tax on both income and wealth; they will use political connections to influence government policy on everything from privatization to taxation. In sum, they have the capacity to promote their own interests, a capacity denied to those lower down the stratification order. However, more significant is the capacity to pass privilege on to succeeding generations. The children of the more privileged members of society will therefore tend to inherit the position of their parents without necessarily having the talents, skill and experience to justify it. A variety of mechanisms make this possible. Money can be passed on to make it possible to buy a house or invest in a business. Connections and networks formed by parents can be useful to children. Probably above all, privileged parents can give educational advantage to their children by ensuring that they go to good schools and universities.

Both arguments can be tested sociologically in the same way because both are in effect about equality of opportunity. One test is the rate of social mobility in a society. If people can move fairly fluidly up and down the class structure, then there is some reason to believe the argument about incentive. If, on the other hand, the structure is sticky and people tend to inherit their class position, then the two arguments look less secure.

What is the evidence about social mobility in the UK? A series of studies over the last thirty years paint a fairly consistent picture.[27] Rates of social mobility do seem to have increased, in that the upper reaches of the class structure have indeed attracted substantial numbers of children of fathers whose own occupations put them towards the bottom. One-third of those in the service class are from working-class origins. Or, to look at it from the other end, one-fifth of those with working-class origins have achieved occupations in the higher classes. On the face of it, that appears to support the meritocracy and incentives arguments. People are not stuck in the social class they were born into but are able to move up if they have talent.

However, it is not quite so straightforward. As I pointed out earlier in the chapter, some occupations, particularly managerial and professional ones, have increased in size considerably in the last fifty years or so. That growth has produced an increased demand for people with appropriate skills and qualifications and that has, so to speak, pulled people up from other social classes, because the upper classes cannot produce enough sons and daughters to meet the demand. So we now have a slightly different key question. Are the chances of a person of working-class origins rising to a service-class position the same as those of a person of service-class origins obtaining that same position?

This is a question about the *relative* chances of upward mobility rather than the *absolute* chances. We have already established that those of working-class origin have a one in five chance of rising to a service-class position. But have they the same chance of obtaining that position as those of more privileged origins? Broadly, the answer is that they do not. The chances of a man from service-class origins ending up in a service-class occupation are seven times greater than those of a man of working-class origins. The class structure, in other words, looks as if it is sticky; service-class people are able to protect the position of their offspring.

This finding about social mobility appears to point to the conclusion that Britain is not a meritocratic society. However, we are not quite there yet. It might, after all, be the case that the children of service-class parents have the abilities that enable them to retain that position, while working-class children do not. The fact that service-class offspring have a better chance of staying service class is therefore simply a reward to their ability and merits. On the face of it, that looks unlikely or, at least, unlikely to the extent required. A suitable test of this possibility is to look at the relationship between class origin, mobility and education. The question that we need to answer is: do children of working-class and service-class origins with similar educational qualifications have a similar chance of attaining service-class positions? If Britain is a meritocratic society, then we should find that people attain their occupational position by virtue of their educational qualifications rather than by their class of origin. Class background should make no difference. In fact, that is not the case. Although those with high educational qualifications have an equal chance of entering service-class occupations whatever their class of origin, those with only middling qualifications do not. Thus, for men with these qualifications, 43 per cent of those with service-class backgrounds end up in service-class occupations while only 15 per cent of those of working-class backgrounds do. Or, to look at it another way, 26 per cent of men with middling qualifications and service-class origins are downwardly mobile into the working class, while 48 per cent of those of working-class origins, and similarly qualified, remain in the working class. The class of origin, in other words, continues to matter, irrespective of ability measured by educational attainment.

In sum, inequality matters for two reasons. First, everybody may accept that *some* degree of inequality is inevitable and that the consequences of any savage reduction in disparities of income would not be tolerable. However, not only is there a substantial degree of inequality of income in modern Britain, the gap between rich and poor is actually increasing. Furthermore, this inequality has a serious impact on the chances in life of the poor. The poor not only lack income, they typically are without employment, are less healthy, less well educated and less well housed, and tend to be without a supportive social network. They are, in other words, deprived of the possibility of participating fully in society.

Second, inequality in some degree would be more tolerable were it possible for people with the ability and talent to achieve a higher income and its benefits. Actually, those in higher social classes are able to protect their children from downward mobility to some extent, even if those children do not have significant educational achievements. After the horrors of the Second World War, the British people thought that a more equal and meritocratic society was to be created. There is still a long way to go.

# Why don't things fall apart?

Things fall apart; the centre cannot hold;
Mere anarchy is loosed upon the world,
The blood-dimmed tide is loosed, and everywhere
The ceremony of innocence is drowned.

W. B. Yeats

## The problem of order

Anxiety seems to suffuse modern life. There are so many things to be worried about. Over the last two or three years, there have been health scares such as the MMR (mumps, measles and rubella) vaccine, GM (genetically modified) food, HIV, MRSA, CJD – a deluge of initials, all of which signify the perils of everyday life. Suddenly, the safety and security of what we take for granted is at risk from forces that we can neither see nor control. We learn to be suspicious of the very food that we put in our mouths. Novel technologies will introduce into our homes – that apparently precious refuge – unsuspected perils. Mobile phones produce brain tumours, videos portray scenes of sex and violence that make the viewer, or the susceptible viewer, turn to violent behaviour. The internet allows our children to meet unsuitable people, virtually or actually. There is danger outside the home, and in the street there is the risk of being mugged. Stock markets will be depressed and pensions will be critically lowered. Global warming will create floods, destroy traditional crops and bring hordes of poisonous insects and refugees to our shores. Our children are at risk from paedophiles. Since sociologists tell us that the risk is greatest from adults who know the children well, we learn to trust nobody. The behaviour of young people, drugged, drunk and violent, is both a threat and a worry. As we saw in chapter 5, work is seen as a source of illness that can prove fatal.

These social anxieties have a number of features in common. They are panics, explosions which appear suddenly, perhaps triggered by an event of some kind, only to subside relatively quickly. Some, it is true, leave residues which can produce flare-ups later on, and others reappear in different forms. They tend to encourage a sense of apocalypse; terrible things are going to happen. At the same time, they exaggerate the degree of risk. For example, the elderly may worry about being attacked in the street, although in fact the chances of a young man being attacked are much higher (a quarter of all violent crime is experienced by young men aged sixteen to twenty-four). The source of anxiety is secret, unseen or disguised; it is an infectious micro-organism, radio-waves, or people who do not look particularly threatening. The media play a critical role in organizing and disseminating the anxiety. For example, on the day that I write this, the Sunday newspapers carry such stories as 'Your child is ill and you need to visit the GP? Sorry . . . not unless you have refugee status'; 'Blood test reveals MMR jab is linked to autism'; 'Why were two new girls put in peril?';[1] 'Teen girls join in race stab attack'.[2] Above all, perhaps, there is a sense of powerlessness. An apparently significant threat, together with an inability to control it, is bound to produce anxiety. Anxieties of this kind are not without historical precedent. Medieval societies, for instance, were plagued by mass movements of people who believed that the world was coming to an end. But their intensity and frequency are particularly modern, not least because of the much greater efficiency of contemporary systems of communication. Some commentators argue that Britain is peculiarly susceptible by comparison with continental Europe or the United States.[3]

Despite the common features of mass anxieties, there are also differences between them. Some, for example, have identifiable perpetrators to blame. A particular group of anxieties, which focus around blame of this kind, are known as moral panics, a term introduced from sociology into everyday speech. Moral panics, as the name implies, involve a moral judgement about the behaviour of a particular group of people. Single parents, those with HIV, paedophiles, young people and drugs, young women and alcohol, travellers, all are recent examples. Moral panics follow roughly the same pattern. Because of a newsworthy event, an issue is identified that appears to pose a threat to the basic values and way of life of society. A group of people are named as responsible and are turned

into 'folk devils'. The media take up the story and extend it by implying that there is a general danger of which this story is but an example.
Influential people (moral entrepreneurs) organize a campaign, forming
associations with like-minded people, lobbying governments and gaining
publicity for their views. Government agencies feel that they have to
respond. The police become more vigilant and make more arrests, judges
impose harsher sentences and governments introduce new legislation,
much of which does not, in fact, make it on to the statute book. There
is a cycle whereby the original event is amplified, sometimes with very
real social effects. Enormous hostility can be shown to the people identified as perpetrators, whether they be homosexuals, travellers, Muslims,
asylum seekers or paediatricians who are mistaken for paedophiles.[4]

Moral panics are responses to the stresses and strains of rapid social
change. In providing an explanation, however, it is important to note
that different groups and institutions – the public, moral entrepreneurs,
the media, government agencies – combine to produce a panic and that
different factors will drive them. Frequently it is the case that those
persons identified as morally lacking or to blame are, in turn, those
whose position in society is changing. So, young people, women, blacks
and the working class have become more visible out of the position that
they had occupied since before the Second World War. For example,
women, especially young women, have entered the job market very
successfully. They compete with men, have stepped outside the roles of
wife and mother, and can afford lifestyles of a radically different kind.
The existing boundaries and conventions have broken, and it is no longer
possible to predict accurately the behaviour of those around. At the same
time, particular groups will have a tendency to be anxious. The elderly,
for example, have usually lost power, prestige and income. They are not
in a position, in other words, to control their world as they used to. It
is not surprising that they will feel threatened by disorder on the streets,
for instance. The media have an interest in finding powerful news stories,
and they cannot afford to neglect them since they are in competition with
each other. Individuals, often public figures but not always so, become
moral entrepreneurs who have an interest in promoting a cause.[5] Government agencies will feel pressured to do something. They cannot afford
to seem inactive in the face of a threat. Any explanation, therefore, is
bound to be complex simply because there are so many actors involved.

The anxieties that I have been describing are all about a disordered
world. The everyday, familiar world appears to be threatened by hostile
others, disease, or transformations in the environment, and commonsense is no longer a good guide to behaviour. We have got used to disorder being the problem and we take for granted that order is the norm
which is being disrupted. For instance, we are used to discussions of

crime in our everyday lives. Why are the streets not safe any more? Why are criminals not punished more severely so that they, and others, will be deterred? Am I safe from burglary? These questions assume that the problem is the existence of crime and criminals. But perhaps this is the wrong problem. The problem is not 'why is there so much crime?' but 'why is there not *more*?' When vandals break every window in a school, it makes the regional television news. But why does this not happen every day? Why do vandals break the windows of a house that has been abandoned but leave untouched those of the clearly inhabited house next door? The problem is not why the world is so disordered but why it is not more so. Or, to put it more generally, why don't things fall apart?

## Coercion

The obvious place to start is with the role of coercion. After all, if someone commits a crime and is caught and found guilty, it is likely that punishment of some kind will follow. It seems an entirely common-sensical position to say that fear of punishment of some kind will keep people from breaking social rules and disturbing social order. It is common for there to be calls to increase punishments for crimes that catch the public's eye on the assumption that, the more that malefactors are caught and punished, the less will crime be committed. On New Year's Eve 2002 in Birmingham, two girls were killed, caught in an exchange of gunfire between two heavily armed groups. There was already considerable public anxiety about the number of guns on the streets, and this incident led to calls for firm action. The government immediately proposed to introduce mandatory sentences for the carrying of a gun (although they went back on it soon afterwards).

Modern governments certainly appear to believe in judicial coercion. Expenditure on the criminal justice system is increasing in the UK. At the end of the 1980s, total spending on the police, prisons and the courts totalled £7.8 billion, of which about 70 per cent went on the police. Ten years later the cost was £10.6 billion.[6] Prison populations in Britain are rising sharply. In 1996, the country had the second highest rate of imprisonment in Europe, at 120 prisoners per 100,000 of the population, exceeded only by Portugal and Spain. In the United States in 2002, 6.6 million people were in the correctional system, in jail, on probation or on parole. This amounts to no fewer than one person in every thirty-two of the population. Of these, 46 per cent are black.[7]

The prison system is the most obvious aspect of the criminal justice system but it is not the only form of coercion exercised by the state. There is an argument that there are new forms of control which have expanded the possibilities of successful – if hidden – coercion. Thus, Stanley Cohen[8] suggests that there have been two transformations in the methods for controlling deviancy in the past two hundred years or so. In the first, the prison becomes the principal means for changing undesirable behaviour. The infliction of pain, which, at worst, is demonstrated in the public execution, is replaced by trying to turn the prisoner away from a life of crime. The state becomes more involved in the control of deviancy as it develops a centralized and bureaucratized system of criminal justice. Lastly, this new system requires an army of trained professionals – experts – to run it. It is important to note that this first change was proposed and implemented for the best of motives. The aim was to rehabilitate the offender, not to punish him, or sometimes her, in a barbaric way. The second transformation was initiated in the 1960s and was based on objections to the way in which a system based on imprisonment had actually worked. The objectors proposed a new system that moved away from institutions and focused correction in the community instead. In the spirit of the 1960s, this proposition was accompanied by calls for a decentralized system and a reduced role for the state and a move away from experts.

Again, this second transformation was proposed for the best of reasons. Prisons were seen as damaging the inmates and as having failed to rehabilitate. The film *The Shawshank Redemption* is a good example of these liberalizing impulses in that it shows the routine violence of prison and the inability of prisoners, when released, to live in the outside world. The criminal justice system was overcontrolling, and professionals had become too intrusive. But, argues Cohen, the actual development of the criminal justice system in the second transformation has actually *expanded* its reach. How has this happened?

The prison population has not declined. In fact, as we have seen, it has been expanding recently. But, at the same time, a system of correction, treatment and supervision in the community has grown up. The result is that more people are being drawn into the net. And it is a less visible system where the boundaries between prison and the community are less clear, as prisoners spend some time 'in the community' after release. Cohen estimated that, between the mid-1960s and the mid-1980s in the United States, the system had doubled its reach, with three-quarters of those supervised being in a community programme. Similar trends are visible in other countries, including Britain.

Community programmes of various sorts, together with imprisonment, are therefore dealing with an increasing number of people who are not serious offenders. But the system is also more orientated to prevention. Schoolteachers and social workers are asked to identify individuals and families who are at risk of offending, and community activities are devised which, although offering help, also effectively supervise. In 2002, the government proposed new mental health legislation in which people diagnosed with personality disorders that were thought to predispose them to violence could be detained in a secure hospital. A newspaper story about the police force in the American state of Delaware makes Cohen's point about modern correction. The force has been compiling a database of people whom they believe are *likely* to break the law. The items on the database are assembled by teams of police cruising high-crime neighbourhoods and stopping, searching and photographing people gathering there.[9] The film *Minority Report* makes the same point. In its fictional world of the future, crimes can be predicted and their perpetrators stopped and incarcerated. Such treatment of people who have not actually committed a crime, but are thought to be about to do so, leads in the story to a mistaken identification of the hero as a criminal.

The expansion of the correctional net described by Cohen is, of course, much helped by the development of appropriate technologies. CCTV cameras, police speed traps, fast searchable databases, offender tagging and identity cards are all means by which the number of people being supervised in one way or another will increase further. The impression given by this view is of a surveillance society in which much of the population, whether they have offended or not, is *watched*.[10]

However, despite this increase in judicial control, this is still only one way in which power is exercised to control people and to try to ensure social order. There is clearly a large number of types of coercion available in every part of society. For example, in chapter 5, I reviewed ways in which workers were controlled by the setting of wages, management supervision and the design of the work process. At the extreme, managements are able to sack workers who infringe the rules that management believe are necessary. Many parents believe that order in a family is maintained by the firm discipline of children. In a quite different way shame and gossip will act as forces of social control. For example, a study of the Punjabi community in Southall in London demonstrated the way that teenagers resented the gossip about them among adults that controlled their behaviour, particularly the relationships between girls and boys.[11]

But as a means of guaranteeing social order, coercion is limited. It is too crude and inefficient. This is for four reasons. First, social control via coercion seems to work best in limited contexts – a workplace, a local community, a prison, for example. But it is not necessarily very transferable across such contexts. So a manager *may* succeed in exercising control over one of her workers. However, that does not stop the worker dropping litter in the street. The more fragmented and mobile a society becomes, the more separated the contexts of social life, the more difficult is the problem of coordinating these contexts. Second, people are good at resisting attempts at control. As we saw in chapter 5, that can be in an open way, as in a strike. It is more likely, however, to be hidden. Workers do not cooperate, they undermine the authority of the manager, or commit acts of sabotage.

The third way in which coercion has its limitations is that stability and order actually depend on the cooperation of all involved, even in social organizations that appear to rely to a considerable extent on coercion. Social order is a kind of collusion between the coercers and the coerced. Again, we have already seen how this operates in work organizations. Employees can disrupt their organizations fairly easily by following rules literally or by acts of organized, if fairly trivial, sabotage. Managers need the cooperation of their workers all the time, simply to make sure that the job is done. An even more apt example is provided by a study of life in a maximum security prison.[12] It is, perhaps, difficult to imagine any organization more coercive than a prison of this type. The structure itself is formidable – 20 foot high walls, floodlighting, wire, a series of steel doors through which people must pass, and watchtowers. The prison staff are all armed; those who man the watchtowers are equipped with shotguns, revolvers and gas grenades. The staff are there to enforce a mass of regulations, many of them apparently petty. Examples are: 'Form by twos when passing through the Center. Keep your place in line unless you are ordered to step out'; 'When walking in line maintain a good posture. Face forwards and keep your hands out of your pockets'; 'When the bell rings for meals, work, or other assignment, turn out your light, see that your water is turned off, and step out of your cell promptly.' In sum, this seems like a powerful structure of control in which the minutest aspects of the prisoners' lives are regimented.

The prison authorities, however, have the greatest difficulty in keeping control and ensuring compliance with the regulations. The inmates just do not behave themselves, and violence, fraud and theft are commonplace in the daily round – and that is just between prisoners. Inmates are expected to work, but officers find it impossible to get them to work *well*. The result is that the quality of work is shoddy, prisoners are apathetic, and sabotage is common. Simple force is ineffective in persuading anyone to perform a task of any complexity. In any case, force can hardly be overwhelming, since the guards are heavily outnumbered by the prisoners.

In fact, the prison only runs at all because, in effect, the prisoners help the guards. The guards actually have a good deal in common with prisoners. They inhabit the same social space and speak the same language. Furthermore, they too suffer from the irritants of power from their superiors. Critically, they turn a blind eye to infractions of the regulations, transmit forbidden information to prisoners, join in criticism of the warden, and ignore elementary security procedures. Guards find it difficult to avoid the claims of reciprocity. They will be evaluated on how troublesome, clean and tidy their section of the prison is, and to be successful they depend on prisoners' cooperation. Furthermore, much of the routine life of a prison is conducted by trusted prisoners on whom, again, the officers come to depend. The result is a delicate balance between guards and prisoners. Guards cannot let too much of their authority slip because they will incur the displeasure of their superiors or of people outside the prison. But they cannot be rigid enforcers because prisoners will not then cooperate. Prisoners have a similar dilemma. In order to preserve any position they must not push the officers too far. In extreme conditions, if this equilibrium is disturbed too much, a prison riot is a possibility.

The fourth respect in which coercion is limited is that social order is actually more fine-grained than the exercise of power or force would alone produce. Two studies will illustrate, in very different ways, what I mean by this.

In the first, Harold Garfinkel, an American sociologist,[13] was interested in how order is produced in everyday life and how the conduct of everyday life in turn sustains order. He conducted an experiment in which he persuaded some of his students to take literally certain entirely conventional conversational gambits. Thus the question 'How are you?' would be greeted with a minute and exact description of bodily states, or with the response 'What do you mean, How am I?' In another version, students would go home and try to behave, say, as a lodger, instead of what they were – son, daughter, wife or husband. Plainly, the point of the experiments was to show what happens when the order of everyday life is experimentally disrupted. In fact, the response on the part of those whose routine was thus disturbed was extraordinarily violent, seemingly disproportionately so. Family members were angry, baffled and worried, and most took a long time to calm down after the experiment was explained to them. Order, therefore, is produced in the interactions of everyday life without anybody realizing it. It is there in the background, self-organized and sustained by the simple routines of daily life. It only becomes obvious that there is order when it is disrupted. This is very much the basis of certain kinds of film. Hitchcock, for example, is a director who makes a good deal of use of the consequences of the sudden disruption of everyday life, perhaps in the case of mistaken identity, as in *North by Northwest*. Films of this kind derive their peculiar terror from the feeling that, if others around one start behaving in a quite different way, then one may not be the person one thought one was. Further poignancy is often added by the contrast between the collapse of the everyday world of the central character and the maintenance of the world of others remote from him. Thus the hero, pursued by nameless and inexplicable terrors, may run through a street crowded with shoppers going about their normal occasions.

It is always tempting to see social order as uncontroversial and apparent disorder as mere anarchy, the absence of rules. Perhaps we all agree that murder is an offence to social order. But we might not all agree that smoking marihuana is. A particular social order is not natural; it is socially constructed and is someone's idea of what is orderly and what is not. Some people may see as anarchic what others perceive as orderly and rule-governed. A study of spectators at football matches illustrates the point.[14]

Newspapers frequently see football crowds as disorderly. Commonly, worse descriptions are used. Whenever trouble breaks out, the perpetrators are described as hooligans or animals. This gives the impression that the events surrounding a match are anarchic by contrast with the match itself, which is highly regulated. It is almost a contrast between nature, red in tooth and claw, and civilization. Actually, the behaviour of football crowds is highly ordered.

The study focuses on those fans who regularly occupy an end of the Oxford United ground and regard this territory as their own. (We have to remember that this study was conducted in the late 1970s, and the geography of football grounds has changed somewhat since.) There is a clear social structure in that defined sub-groups occupy particular parts of the end. The Rowdies are distinguished by their dress – the 'aggro outfit' – their use of banners and scarves and the noise they make. Their ages range from twelve to seventeen. The Town Boys are older, between sixteen and twenty-five, quieter and dressed unremarkably. There is also a group of young children with an average age of about ten. The authors distinguish three other groups, one consisting of young men the same age as the Rowdies but characterized by having a history of arrests, probation and care orders. The other two groups are much less distinct and are regarded scornfully by the others as being 'part-time'. A career is discernible in which the young children become Rowdies over time and Rowdies, in turn, migrate to the Town Boys' patch. The relationships between the groups are reminiscent of the way that marihuana users and punks form cultures which establish identity, described in chapter 2.

The Rowdies are those most likely to be regarded by those in authority as football hooligans. Their activities, however, are highly ordered and rule-governed. There is a division of labour within the group which the Rowdies themselves recognize. Some are organizers, some chant, some lead fights. Even the fighting with visiting supporters from other clubs is highly ritualized and orderly. Invasions of territory are invitations to fight, and there are apparent rules for the issue and acceptance of a challenge. There has to be a reason for a fight – the wearing of a team scarf, for instance. Fights, in other words, do not start up randomly but occur in circumstances which the fans regard as legitimating their actions. Furthermore, the extent of the fight is controlled. It is rare for anybody to be seriously hurt, and most encounters are settled without any exchange of blows but rather a great deal of running about. Indeed, the point seems to be to get your opponent to run away. Now, the claim that this behaviour is governed by rules is not necessarily to excuse it. It is rather to argue that social life is patterned and orderly at football grounds, just as in the families that Garfinkel investigated.

## Common values

Force works in certain circumstances, but it is not a particularly efficient means of securing order. But perhaps societies do not need the exercise of force, or do so only in the most extreme of conditions, because of the values that the members of society hold. People are restrained from disorderly acts because they believe them to be wrong and know that their neighbours think so too. In addition, they may believe that those who give orders have the right to do so.

This idea has been an influential one in sociology. Its corollary – that the present discontents of society stem from a disorder which results from the failure of common moral beliefs – is also a commonplace of modern public debate. Followers of this line of reasoning argue that all would be well if only firm moral convictions were taught and followed. Such a view is correct to the extent that, if common values about the right way to behave are to work in maintaining social order, then they have to be taught and learned. They have to be deeply rooted so that individuals literally see no other way of behaving. These common values will work in such a way that individuals are not faced with choices on which they ponder. They are so fundamental that people do not need to choose. They just act in accordance with those values without further reflection. Individuals, in other words, must have *internalized* the common values; they must have made them part of their very identity. Acting in conformity with embedded common values therefore happens without further reflection; it is just part of the ebb and flow of everyday life. Such a degree of internalization would indicate that, were deeprooted common values to be challenged, individuals would not just react with outrage. They would also be profoundly shocked and disorientated, for their everyday world would have turned upside down.

Now, to some extent, common values do work like that in everyday life. Some values are so basic that they are entirely taken for granted and surface only when they are disrupted. Child abuse is a good example of this. Whenever children are abused, or even murdered, public outrage is such that it is clear that there is a fundamental value here that is being transgressed. (Although it is also worth remembering the argument of chapter 3 that this attitude depends on a particular view of childhood, which, however deeply rooted and apparently natural, is actually socially constructed.) It is also possible to read the Garfinkel experiments that I mentioned earlier in the same way. People involved in a close relationship with each other operate to a set of common values that give order and structure to their daily lives. These values are so taken for granted that their breach leads to an apparently disproportionate reaction. However, the proposition that people internalize values in this way requires a very efficient process of *socialization*. That is, there has to be an effective teaching and learning process. Normally, socialization is divided into two main phases. The first, primary socialization, takes place during infancy. Most of the learning takes place as a result of the interaction between the infant and adults. It is during this phase that we acquire the fundamentals about the culture and organization of the groups to which we belong. Not least, we learn the importance of relating to others and, throughout life, we are conscious of others' views and opinions, even when they are not present. Secondary socialization takes place among equals, playmates, brothers and sisters and school friends, rather than between adult and child. Clearly, socialization involving equals continues lifelong, but the assumption is that the earlier years will be most significant in the acquisition of important values.

Is the socialization process effective enough to allow individuals fully to internalize common values? It is worth noting in passing that the possibility that there could be a ruthlessly efficient socialization process very much worries those who are as concerned about individual freedom as they are about social order. These worries frequently have fictional representation. Orwell, Kafka and Huxley all wrote novels in which an individual who does not conform effectively demonstrates how conformist most others are. In these images force is unnecessary. Social order is achieved by control of the mind, not of the body. For many, therefore, the problem is rather more the prospect of an overordered society in which the individual effectively *volunteers* to be unfree.

Fortunately, the actual process of learning is not remotely as effective as that. Individuals may very well learn values at their parents' knees. But they learn those values that their parents teach, and they may very well be different from those of the parents in the next community. In a fragmented society, these potential conflicts will be that much more severe. Furthermore, the growing child may actually be subjected to contradictory sources of social learning. Famously, adolescent peer groups will socialize their members into values and behaviour that shock the parents concerned. The socialization process, in other words, is not unified. In that sense, it reflects society well, but is not likely to result in an unfragmented set of common values across society. At the best, it will produce a certain coherence within fairly narrowly defined social contexts – the family, the teenage group, for example. But there is no guarantee that these separate contexts will themselves cohere together.

Similar conclusions may be reached by looking at the other end of the socialization process – the values expressed by adults. If one asks people about their moral beliefs, there certainly are some values on which there appears to be substantial agreement. One study discovered, for example, that people have stricter and more intolerant moral attitudes to legal issues, such as murder or theft, than they have towards more private concerns, such as homosexuality or divorce.[15] However, this turns out not to be such a unanimity of view, since different social groups within the population have very different moral outlooks. In general, younger people are more liberal and tolerant than their elders. They favour more indulgent treatment of those found breaking the law and greater toleration of those whose behaviour flouts convention. Those who have a religious commitment generally have a stricter outlook on all moral questions. Working-class people tend to be less tolerant towards breaches of convention in personal and private matters than the middle class, who are, in turn, stricter in their attitudes to those who break the law.

There is a further difficulty in that expressed moral beliefs may vary between different social contexts. They are not like some hard nut that people carry around with them and produce in the same form when the occasion demands. Rather, they are context-dependent; what people will say, what values they hold dear, and how they behave depends to some extent on who they are with and what the peculiarities of the situation are. One way in which this emerges is in the often puzzling connection between moral belief and moral conduct. What people say they believe does not always seem to be apparent in the way that they behave. This disjunction does not arise out of any hypocrisy or weakness in which people say one thing and do another. It is more that, in real social situations, beliefs conflict, and it is not clear what action should follow. For example, in one study the authors were initially surprised to find that, while their interviewees disapproved of unofficial strikes, many had a history of taking part in them or went on to participate in unofficial action subsequently.[16]

## Altruism, exchange and trust

Human beings in any society are linked together in an intricate network of relationships of give and take. Such relationships are obviously of different kinds. At work, for example, a secretary may agree to cover for her colleague for a time in exchange for a similar favour on another occasion. A grandmother may look after her grandson for a day every week while her son works. In this case, there is no *explicit* exchange of favours. The grandmother simply thinks that it is her duty and part of being a mother. Nevertheless, it would be surprising if her son did not cut her hedge or mend her car once in a while. Quite a lot of people in Britain volunteer to give blood on a regular basis. They do so because they believe that is part of their contribution to the welfare of others. This, then, looks like an act of pure altruism in that the donor does not know, and never will know, the person who eventually receives their blood and they do not expect any recompense.

Exchanges such as these are special cases of a general interdependency between members of society. In order for anyone to pursue his or her own interests, or indeed to exist as a member of society, the co-operation of other people is necessary. People are systematically involved in a series of exchanges. That much is obvious. Some of the clearest examples of the way that these exchanges work in constructing interdependence come from the sphere of economic behaviour. A simple example is the exchange between employer and worker of wages for labour. The exchange serves the interests of both parties. In a more complex way, a motor car production line is a series of interdependencies characterized by a set of exchanges. Specialized producers are brought together to supply parts which are then assembled by workers who will work on only part of the car. The process as a whole is an assembly of interdependent parts. It is possible to describe the entire economic system in a similar way. It is at least plausible to see such interdependence founded in exchanges as a source of social order. Everybody has an interest in keeping the system going to achieve their own objectives. And their interest extends beyond their immediate context since breakdowns in exchanges anywhere will put the whole system at risk.

Social life is, of course, not restricted to economic transactions. To show how exchanges and interdependence work in other spheres I turn to two quite different studies.

In the United Kingdom, the supply of blood for transfusion comes largely from unpaid donors. The author of a study of the system of blood supply conducted in the late 1960s, Richard Titmuss, was interested in how and why the system differed from the one operating in the United

States, which was based largely on paying donors.[17] He concluded that supply by voluntary donation produces cheaper and purer blood in larger quantities. This is simply because, in the United States, donors are poor and are likely to carry diseases, which results in a quantity of blood being thrown away.

Why are the British apparently altruistic in giving blood? In essence, blood donors in Britain are making a gift. Now, in early, so-called primitive societies, gift-giving is very important. For example, in the tribal societies of the North American Indians gifts circulate freely. They will be reciprocated eventually, although the reciprocation can take time. More significant is the *obligation* to give. In all that anthropologists write about gifts, there is a vivid sense of the pervasiveness of the social obligation and the power of the sanctions that apply to defaulters – dishonour, shame and guilt. Gift exchanges of this kind bind these societies together morally. Now, obviously, the giving of blood in our society is quite different from those gifts made in tribal societies. There are no obvious penalties for not giving, no certainty of receiving a gift back, in fact no expectation of it, and, probably most important, the giver and the receiver are strangers. So, what does motivate blood donors in Britain? Is there some modern equivalent of the moral obligation of tribal societies? Titmuss asked donors about that. He concluded that gift exchanges have a fundamental importance in modern societies in preserving the harmony of a civilized life. Practically all of the donors asked by Titmuss employed a *moral* vocabulary to explain their reasons for giving blood; they did not expect to be entirely self-interested. Furthermore, their social universe was not confined to their family or friends; it also included total strangers. None of the answers was purely altruistic. There was always some sense of obligation, approval or interest, some awareness of the need and purpose of the gift, and even some notion of possibly needing a transfusion oneself.

For some time in Britain there has been a debate about family obligation. As governments increasingly prove reluctant to fund a welfare system that will care for people in old age, attention turns to the role of the family in serving that function. A study of family obligation by Finch and Mason[18] did not find any very general feeling that the family should be the first port of call for any family member who wants or needs help. For example, in response to the proposition 'Children have no obligation to look after their parents when they are old', 58 per cent of the sample thought that there was an obligation and 39 per cent thought that there was not. Despite this absence of consensus, kinship relations remain very important in the flows of support and help throughout a person's life. Almost every person interviewed by Finch and Mason had given or received financial help, or both, and a whole range of other kinds of help, including emotional support and practical assistance, were involved as well.

In all these flows of support, there was a strong moral belief in reciprocity – the expectation that, if one gives help, it will be returned at some time. The question of balance is very important so that one party is not permanently indebted to another. Sometimes balance is achieved by direct repayment, as in the case of a loan, for example. Much more commonly, the repayment is indirect; wallpaper hanging is exchanged for home-baking, for instance. The difficulty with indirect exchanges of this kind is fixing on an appropriate rate of exchange – how much gardening for how much childcare – which will avoid the risk of imbalance in the exchange. Given the absence of firm and widely agreed conventions, together with the difficulty of establishing rates of exchange, most families become involved in a protracted process of negotiation which is very frequently formalized in a family discussion. As a result of these negotiations, particular individuals come to develop lasting commitments to each other over time. The relationship of mutual support continues to the point when the mother goes to live with her son and his family.

The negotiations between family members consist of both material and moral exchanges, and they create moral identities for each person involved. Finch and Mason describe this as 'moral baggage' which gets carried forward over time and is reshaped through repeated negotiations. Central to the construction of moral identities is the idea of reputation, and one way of exploring this is to look at how people see the tension between asking for and receiving help. In general, respondents concluded that asking for help was not wrong in all circumstances. At the same time, it is clear that it is not desirable for anyone to be in a position where they have to ask, so potential donors have a duty to take the initiative and offer first. This is because, if recipients ask, their moral identities are compromised; they appear dependent or greedy.

Within these constraints, individuals will acquire different moral reputations, and there is a shared image of each person within the kin group. Some will be seen as generous with time and money. One son described his mother in this way:

> I thank the Lord for my mum and dad every day. The amount of times that my mum and dad's helped me out, you know. Especially to have someone like my mum to lean on. I don't know how I'd feel – I mean obviously at some time in the future she's going to die. And I don't know how I'll take it.[19]

Unfavourable reputations can be equally persistent. A son will get defined as someone who is always borrowing money or an uncle cast in the role of the family black sheep. These images are important because they determine how individuals behave towards one another. In particular, reputations provide a structure for negotiations about assistance. People will know whom to go to for assistance, who is reliable, and who is good at rendering particular kinds of help.

Titmuss's study of blood donation and Finch and Mason's study of family obligation are both concerned with exchange and interdependency. Those who offer their blood and those who give support to fellow family members know that there is an exchange. There is reciprocity. True, this reciprocity is not an explicit feature of each and every act of exchange. Actually, to make it explicit would ruin the basis for the relationship. Nonetheless, when interviewed, people are conscious of the reciprocal basis on which they act. The reciprocity forges the interdependence. The idea of the gift sums this up well, as Titmuss indicated. People feel obligated to make gifts and to receive them, they feel that it is morally right to do so, and, since the making of gifts almost always involves reciprocity, the links between people are reinforced.

It is also clear that there is a *moral* basis for these exchanges. They are not crude transactions. Interviewees used a moral language to describe their own actions and those of others. And this is not a smokescreen, for the moral commitments determine the actions that form the long-term exchanges. Moral commitment, in other words, is inseparably intertwined with the exchanges that make for interdependence and orderliness. And this crucial interconnection is well understood even by those who advocate a society, and sets of exchanges, based entirely on free-market principles without any moral interference from the state. Adam Smith, for example, always taken as the original apostle of the free market in the eighteenth century, believed that markets would not operate without a firm moral basis.[20] One way of demonstrating these connections is to note the nature of trust. Most of the transactions in which we engage in everyday life are founded in trust. When buying a pint of milk at the corner shop, we trust that the milk is fresh and that we have been given the right change. The family exchanges described by Finch and Mason are long-term relationships in which it is necessary that people trust each other. Paradoxically, even the collusion between prison officers and prisoners discussed earlier in this chapter depends on trust. Trust provides the basis upon which transactions can take place at all. Apart from anything else, it is a cheap and efficient way to get through the day. Imagine how much time it would take to suspend trust and examine each of our transactions in detail. At the same time, trust is a *moral* phenomenon. It implies a declaration of faith, a belief in the worthiness of others, which potentially exposes to risk.[21]

Social order is, therefore, rather like a three-legged stool. Coercion, moral commitments and interdependency are all necessarily intertwined in producing orderliness in the social world. Disturb the balances between them and the system as a whole may become wobbly. The maintenance of balance, of equilibrium, is a movement that goes on, relatively unnoticed, under the surface of social life. It demands a good deal of effort but it is effort that we take for granted. Unless savagely disrupted, social order is simply *there*.

# Has the magic gone?

O for a life of sensations rather than of thoughts!

John Keats

When most people set out to make a chocolate cake they use a recipe; they do not simply dump all the ingredients into a bowl and hope for the best. They use precisely measured quantities, follow a series of steps in a particular order, and bake at the right temperature for a given time. It is a calculated, precise, planned and efficient process, even if the end product is a rock-hard and blackened slab.[1]

In modern times, many families, especially large families, have members distributed all over the world. One of the ways everybody stays in touch is to have reunions, perhaps organized around a major birthday. Whoever is responsible for organizing such events has to plan carefully. Dates and times have to be agreed, hotels booked, reminders sent. The various steps have to be coordinated in time and space, and tasks have to be discharged in a set sequence.

Over the last twenty years or so, body maintenance has become a major preoccupation of many people in Western countries. A worry about being too fat leads to a careful scrutiny of the calorie content of everything we eat. Helpful books appear which tell you exactly how many calories there are in a pizza with mushrooms in Pizza Express. Commercial gyms spring up, all equipped with strange machines which measure the effort we put in and allow us to rack up personal best times.

We are enjoined to walk – rapidly – for thirty minutes at least five times a week. Meanwhile we become fatter and less fit.

These distinctive activities of everyday life have a number of features in common. They all involve planning – thinking ahead and connecting items in a sequence. They are efficient – they use as little resource as possible to reach objectives. They involve measurement and calculation. And they all run the risk of ruining a pleasurable human experience. The cake can be so precisely measured that any possibility of innovation – adding more chocolate, for instance – is suppressed. An intimate conversation between two long-separated cousins has to be interrupted because the schedule says that it is now time to guess which adult relative was that baby in old family photographs. Exercise is no longer the pleasure of running free with hair streaming in the wind; it is the grind of doing ten laps in thirty minutes.

Making a chocolate cake, planning a party and adopting a regime of exercise are all examples of *rationalization*.[2] One might define rationalization as that process that encourages rational action, that is, action that strives to adopt the most efficient means to reach a given objective. One can often understand what something is by seeing what it is not. So, rational action is not action carried out because it has always been done that way. It is not spontaneous action without forethought. It is not action proceeding from some compelling emotion. It is not action determined by moral, spiritual or religious considerations. The argument to be explored in this chapter is that rationalization understood in this way is an all-pervasive social process. It is so pervasive that it has formed everyday life as a series of background assumptions that are rarely questioned.

## Measurement and calculation

I want to travel from John O'Groats to Land's End. Now, if I were not being rational about this objective, I would simply set off and drive down the nearest road. In our society that would be seen as simply foolish, the action of a madman or perhaps of someone with too much time and money. The rational course of action would be to work out how to get there with the least expenditure of effort. I would need to *measure* – how many miles is it by different road routes, how much will it cost by different means of transport, how much time will I have to spend. I then have to *calculate* the best transport solution. My idea of what is best might be expressed in terms of minimizing the time that I will spend, or the cost in money, or perhaps some other resource such as emotional stress. Note that being rational is not to do with the nature of the objective itself. One may well regard a wish to travel from John O'Groats to Land's End as lacking in originality or sense, but the rationality or otherwise of the objective is quite different from the means that I adopt to realize that objective.[3]

Calculation and its associated measurements are crucial to the process of rationalization. Indeed, measurement and quantification seem to infest every nook and cranny of modern life. One cannot watch a game of football on television without having a whole range of statistics flashed up on the screen. Choosing a university is allegedly made easier by having league tables of higher education institutions. Hospitals have every aspect of their activities measured, from waiting lists to mortality rates from operations.

Time and money are probably the most widespread ways of measuring human activities. Most people carry a watch and refer to it frequently. It would be fairly difficult to conduct a planned and rational everyday life without timed arrangements. But the constant reference to precisely measured time is actually a relatively modern phenomenon. Thus, one may contrast modern societies that are clock-orientated to pre-modern ones that are task-orientated.[4] In the former, the routines of life are measured by the clock. For example, people work for a given period of time each day. In task-orientated societies, on the other hand, people attend to the task before them, taking in the harvest, or lambing, until it is completed. In such societies, to the extent that time is relevant at all, it is not very precise. Eighteenth-century treatises on agriculture might talk about a field of corn taking perhaps a day to harvest or maybe two if it was wet. Such relative vagueness about time persisted even in nineteenth-century railway timetables. Although the measurement of time is clearly necessary for a rational railway system – a lesson that has not been learned even now – the introduction of timetables had to cope with the fact that different towns in the United Kingdom ran to different time-zones. Even as late as 1841, the Great Western Railway timetable contained the following:

> London time is kept at all stations on the railway, which is about 4 minutes earlier than Reading time; 5 minutes before Cirencester time; 8 minutes before Chippenham time; and 14 minutes before Bridgewater time.[5]

The clock is tyrannical. It imposes a form of control on us which is very difficult to avoid. That is obvious at work if for no other reason than that people are paid by the hour, day, week or month and are expected to appear at work at a particular time. However, it invades leisure as well. At the least, television programmes run at specific times and squash courts have to be booked. More seriously, the intrusion of time-management into our spare time seems ironically to be related to the *lack* of time for leisure. One theorist of leisure has gone as far as to claim that what has increased, especially in the last twenty years, is anti-leisure, activity which is undertaken compulsively, as a means to an end, from a perception of necessity, with a high degree of externally imposed constraints, with considerable anxiety, with a high degree of time-consciousness and with the minimum of personal autonomy. Leisure is rationalized just as work is. We like to think of our leisure as a relaxation, as a source of pleasure, as an antidote to work. But a modern, time-governed leisure is anything but that. It is highly organized, planned and taken so *seriously*. Commercial sports centres even look like factories, with rows of exercise machines, each of which is loaded with measuring devices. As I argued earlier, modern sport is so often not the spontaneous enjoyment of physical exercise. It is undertaken with a *purpose* – as a means to an end – to get fit or thin.

In the calculation of the most efficient means of achieving objectives there are few more effective means of measurement than money. Our very language is saturated with expressions indicative of the importance of money as a measuring device. So we say 'time is money'; we talk of 'profiting' from an experience; when we take risks we say 'in for a penny, in for a pound'.

The use of metaphors of this kind indicates that money is a pervasive and unconsciously used yardstick, a means of assessing human experience. It even invades the realms of aesthetic and moral judgement. For example, comparative aesthetic judgements are often very difficult to make because most people lack the experience, language and conceptual apparatus to make them. Such questions as: why is this poem doggerel and this not? Why is this picture so much better than that? Why is this piece of pottery the work of an artist while that one is produced by a craftsman? tend to be answerable only with a technical vocabulary. But, attach financial values to these items and they become measurable and comparable. In an exhibition of studio pottery which attaches prices to each piece, or in a show in which pictures, apparently similar, but which have very different auction prices, are placed side by side, people are able to engage in aesthetic debate. The question then becomes: why is this picture by Roger Fry worth so much less than this one by Paul Cezanne, despite their apparent similarity of treatment and of subject and the fact that they were painted at roughly the same time? Armed with a device – money – that makes for comparison, those present at the show are able to make a better stab at answering that question.[6]

One way of exploring the pervasiveness of money as a form of measurement is to utilize the idea of *commodification*. The proposition here is that, over time, more and more objects, human experiences and activities have a monetary value attached to them so that they can be traded in a market of some kind. In the earlier stages of human history, people produced things for their own use. A family would grow its own food and manufacture any tools that they needed. As societies developed, people bartered with each other, perhaps exchanging food surplus to their own requirements. Gradually markets appeared where such bartering could be made easier, and money became used as a medium of exchange. Eventually, people were producing things, not for their own use directly, but to sell in a market. They were producing *commodities*.[7] The outcome is that, in modern societies, anything can potentially be a commodity, capable of having a monetary value attached to it and of being bought and sold. So courts of law place a price on human life as a matter of routine; in many countries there is a trade in human organs; and there is an active current debate as to the extent to which private companies can be said to own human genes which may have commercial possibilities. An illustration of this argument is provided by a study of the commodification of human emotion by Arlie Hochschild.[8]

*The Managed Heart* is a study of airline stewardesses or flight attendants. Airlines have since the 1970s been very competitive with one another. One of the most important ways in which they compete is in the quality of their service. The most important part of the service is the behaviour of the cabin staff, since passengers have far more contact with them than with any other airline employee. Flight attendants have to be friendly, unfailingly courteous and treat passengers as if they were friends or relatives. A vital part of the job is to display the appropriate emotions; the airline is, in effect, selling emotions, and flight attendants are engaged in what the author calls *emotional labour*. Airlines are not alone in this. As modern economic life switches from manufacturing things to providing services, so emotional labour becomes more important. Hochschild estimates that one-third of American workers are thus engaged.

The point is, of course, that the airlines are deliberately engineering all this; they are commodifying people's private emotions. Thus in the intensive training session, a trainer addresses the trainees: 'Now girls, I want you to go out there and really smile. Your smile is your biggest asset. I want you to go out there and use it. Smile. *Really* smile. Really *lay* it on.'[9] Flight attendants have to treat passengers as if they were in their living room. Here is one speaking: 'You think how the new person resembles someone you know. You see your sister's eyes in someone sitting at that seat. That makes you want to put out for them. I like to think of the cabin as the living room of my own home.'[10] Sincerity is highly valued in the company; attendants are critical of those who put on fake friendliness: 'What the passengers want is real people. They're tired of that empty pretty face.'[11] The selection of flight attendants must of course reflect these demands. For example, the manual issued to applicant attendants before they attend interview, under the heading 'Appearance', says that facial expressions should be 'sincere' and 'unaffected'. One should have a 'modest but friendly smile' and be 'generally alert, attentive, not overly aggressive, but not reticent either'. Under 'Mannerisms', sub-heading 'Friendliness', it is suggested that a successful candidate must be 'outgoing but not effusive' and 'vivacious but not effervescent'.

It's fairly obvious what the company is after. As one trainer says, 'You're selling yourself... We're in the business of selling ourselves, right?'[12] What, however, is the effect of this emotional labour on the attendants themselves? How are private feelings transmuted into public labour? Attendants experience considerable difficulty in coming down into private life after public displays. After all, where is the real self, where is the real, *private* self, if it has been publicly displayed for commercial gain and without the adequate depth of feeling? The result is that attendants have to *manage* their feelings. In order to present the required warm emotions, they have to contain their often justified anger. In order for emotions to be *sold*, they have to be *managed* by the attendants.

This emotional labour – the transmutation of private feelings into public labour – can also be a source of friction between company and attendants. Back to smiling. In the flight attendant's work, smiling is separated from its usual function, which is to express a personal feeling, and is attached to another one – expressing a company feeling. The company is constantly trying to get them to up the rate of work. 'The company exhorts them to smile more and "more sincerely", at an increasing number of passengers. The workers respond to the speed-up with a slow-down; they smile less broadly, with a quick release and no sparkle in the eye, thus dimming the company's message to the people. It is a war of smiles.'[13] A battle over emotion can develop in much the same way as the slow-downs in the clothing factory described in chapter 5.

## Efficiency and control

Rationalization is a habit of mind and a set of practices which seek the most efficient means to reach a given objective. To the rationalized mind, one of the most obvious ways to be efficient when faced by a task of any degree of complexity is to divide up the task into a number of steps – to introduce a division of labour. This is clearest of all for work processes, and the classical account of the division of labour at work was provided by the eighteenth-century economist Adam Smith.

In Adam Smith's book *The Wealth of Nations*,[14] there is an analysis of the making of pins. At one time, the making of pins was almost a craft. A craftsman made the whole pin, from preparing the wire, cutting and sharpening it, putting on the head and so on. But gradually, as the scale of manufacture increased, the stages of pin-making became separated out, and workers became specialized in completing each stage. One would sharpen all the pins, while another put on all the heads. Now, this degree of specialization is efficient, that is, it achieves the result with the minimum deployment of resources. It does so for two reasons. First, if people specialize in any one task, they become adept at it and work more efficiently at it. They become more skilled at less and less. So, if you concentrate on pin sharpening, you are more productive than if you have to bother with putting the heads on as well. Second, craftsmen are more expensive to hire than labourers. People who can make a whole pin are relatively skilled and have been relatively more highly trained. Pin sharpeners, on the other hand, are not so skilled and consequently are less highly paid. Such a division of labour can be applied to any industrial process and can also be further refined so that the steps become smaller and smaller and workers more and more specialized.

As I pointed out when discussing bureaucracy in chapter 5, it is possible to introduce division of labour of this kind into any human activity. It is as much a question of scale as anything else. For activities which are not repeated very often, it may not be worth the effort of designing a division of labour. The arrangement of a family reunion described at the beginning of this chapter would be a case in point. For specialized cars produced in very small numbers, a full-scale production line is not cost-effective, and it will be cheaper to employ more highly skilled workers to assemble fairly large parts of the car. However, generally, the rationalizing tendency to greater efficiency through increased division of labour is so pervasive that it seems perfectly natural. Our daily life seems to be run on this principle. For example, if you want to visit the doctor, you ring up the receptionist and make an appointment. The doctor recommends a course of treatment and a visit to a specialist at the local hospital. You visit the pharmacist to fill a prescription and make an appointment with the hospital specialist. The specialist runs a clinic in which she is assisted by nurses, other doctors and administrative staff. Having examined you, she may well need to call in the further help of other doctors and health professionals – radiographers or physiotherapists, for example. This often lengthy process then involves a series of steps each of which is staffed by someone different, trained in a specialized way.

Rationalization of this kind seems entirely natural, the only way to do things. However, it is actually a social achievement. The development of military power in Europe in the sixteenth and seventeenth centuries provides a good example of this point.[15] In the period before this, armies were composed of a relatively ill-disciplined body of men, largely mercenaries, commanded by aristocrats, appointed largely by patronage, with no training in warfare and with little systematic loyalty to the state. They developed into a disciplined body organized carefully into sub-units with distinct functions. The state funded and equipped them, and the subservience to the interests of the state was established and sustained by such symbolic means as the wearing of uniform. The leadership was professionalized and a military bureaucracy gradually developed. The process of rationalization extended down to the small-scale. Not only was the army organized tactically into small units which were expected to coordinate with each other, so also was the behaviour of the individual soldier regulated by a system of drill and discipline. Thus, in the seventeenth and eighteenth centuries it was realized that firepower was critical. The simple act of loading and firing a gun was broken down into a series of steps, each of which was learned in detail. On receipt of an order, all soldiers in a unit would go through the same series of steps, and disciplined and coordinated fire was the result.

It is tempting to see greater efficiency achieved through the division of labour as an unalloyed benefit. However, what is efficient from one person's view may not be from another's. Thus, workers on a production line may see the costs that specialization entails. Here, for example, is a Ford worker speaking about his job:

> It's the most boring job in the world. It's the same thing over and over again. There's no change in it, it wears you out. It makes you awful tired. It slows your thinking right down. There's no need to think. It's just a formality. You just carry on. You just endure it for the money. That's what we're paid for – to endure the boredom of it. If I had the chance to move I'd move right away. It's the conditions here. Ford class you more as a machine than men. They're on top of you all the time. They expect you to work every minute of the day. The atmosphere you get in here is so completely false. Everyone is so downcast and fed up.[16]

Similarly, the patient may feel that they are carrying a substantial part of the cost in the increasing division of labour in medical practice in that a great deal of time and emotional energy is expended in going from one practitioner to another. Of course, there are advantages for the patient in medical specialization. The evidence shows, for example, that surgeons who specialize in breast cancer surgery have much better results than those who may perform only a few such operations per year. There are also disadvantages in that the patient is not being treated as a whole person. For example, a patient with more than one condition may receive treatment from different practitioners for each. Unless their treatment as a whole is considered, there is a risk that they may be put on too many drugs or that these may interfere with each other.

Hidden in the machinery of rationalization is *control*. In the production, let us say, of chairs, managers wish to ensure that there is a flow of product of a consistent quality. This is much easier in a planned and specialized system of production. If every chair was assembled completely by individual craftsmen, it would be that much more difficult to guarantee that all chairs in a set were of the same quality. Similarly, it is easier to control the workers. The craftsman who is relatively unspecialized has some independence because he controls the whole of the production of an item. The specialized labourer, on the other hand, has control over only one element of the entire process. He can easily be replaced or his work circumvented. In work environments with a high division of labour, workers can only resist if they organize together.

But rationalization has a rather more intimate and general relationship with control. In the previous chapter I discussed the way in which social order might be maintained not so much by physical punishment as by a process of surveillance. The contrast between punishment and surveillance is well put by Michel Foucault.[17] His book *Discipline and Punish* opens with the description by a contemporary Parisian of a public execution in 1757. The plan for the execution was as follows. The criminal was to be placed in a cart dressed only in a shirt, taken to a scaffold in a public place, where the executioner was to tear at his body with red-hot pincers; his right hand which committed the murder would be burnt with sulphur; his wounds would have molten lead, boiling oil, burning resin, wax and sulphur poured over them. Then his body would be drawn and quartered, consumed by fire and reduced to ashes, and his ashes thrown to the winds. Unfortunately all did not go entirely to plan. The executioner was not very strong and was incompetent with the red-hot pincers. The sulphur did not burn strongly enough. Even the drawing and quartering did not succeed very well, and eventually six horses were required to perform the task. The result was that the prisoner was caused a certain amount of pain.

Eighty years later than this spectacle of public torture, another Parisian was describing a set of rules for young prisoners. This began with article 17: 'The prisoners' day will begin at six in the morning and five in summer. They will work for nine hours a day throughout the year. Two hours a day will be devoted to instruction. Work and the day will end at nine o'clock in winter and eight in summer.' And it finished with article 28: 'At half-past seven in summer, half-past eight in winter, the prisoners must be back in their cells after the washing of hands and the inspection of clothes in the courtyard; at the first drum-roll, they must undress, and at the second get into bed. The cell doors are closed and the supervisors go the rounds in the corridors to ensure order and silence.'[18]

There is only an eighty-year gap between these two descriptions. Yet the first is an unspeakable barbarism to modern eyes and ears. The latter, on the other hand, is at least a recognizably modern form of punishment. As Foucault says, first a public execution, second a timetable.

Foucault is not just interested in punishment for its own sake. But, for him, the way in which societies punish their deviants is an indication of the way that they discipline and control *all* their members. Physical coercion has been replaced by surveillance – a process by which people are recorded, filed, numbered and, literally, watched. As a result, each one of us has become visible and potentially controllable. Modern societies have a string of methods to identify us. We have names, our birthdays are important to us, we have a whole set of numbers attached to us – national insurance numbers, bank account numbers, computer passwords. Without these forms of identification we could do very little in modern society. We could not visit the doctor, open a bank account or obtain any state benefit. Our identity makes us *identifiable*. And there is, of course, a proposal to create a single master number which would make the whole process that much more efficient. All these are features of rationalization, the relentless pursuit of the most efficient means.

## Moral decline and disenchantment

We are used to thinking of efficiency and rationality as good things. Inefficiency, after all, will squander resources that could be dedicated to other uses. I have already argued that there is a price for the gains of rationalization which has the potential for the restriction of human freedom. There may be a darker side still, however. To show what this might mean, I turn to a study of the Holocaust by Zygmunt Bauman.[19]

Bauman argues that most people think about the Holocaust in one of two ways. First, it was a uniquely Jewish event, determined by the particular character of the Jewish people as outsiders without a nation of their own. Second, it was an irrational moment in history perpetrated by madmen who had reverted to some savage or animal past. For both explanations, the murder of 6 million Jews was a pathological event unlikely to be repeated. Bauman points to some difficulties with these views. For example, he notes that the soldiers who operated the death camps were not madmen. In fact the SS went to some trouble to weed out men who appeared too enthusiastic. Far from being a unique event, Bauman argues that, although nothing on the same scale has happened since the Second World War, events betraying the same habits of mind happen every day. However, he really wants to say something much more radical. He argues that the Holocaust was an outcome of the rationalizing processes so characteristic of Western civilization. In this sense, it is far from irrational, and that is what makes it so especially terrifying.

What can he mean by this? What he means, above all, is that the Holocaust was the outcome of modern *bureaucratic* processes. Indeed it could not have come about *without* modern bureaucracy. It required careful planning, designing proper technology and technical equipment, budgeting, calculating and mobilizing necessary resources. The bureaucrats were given a problem to solve – the removal of the Jews from Germany – and so they set about it rationally, adopting the most efficient means to that end. As a historian of the Holocaust has written:

> [Auschwitz] was also a mundane extension of the modern factory system. Rather than producing goods, the raw material was human beings and the end-product was death, so many units per day marked carefully on the manager's production charts . . . The brilliantly organized railroad grid of modern Europe carried a new kind of raw material to the factories. It did so in the same manner as with other cargo . . . Engineers designed the crematoria; managers designed the system of bureaucracy that worked with a zest and efficiency more backward nations would envy.[20]

So, for Bauman, the Holocaust was not a failure of rationality; rather it was a triumph. It was not a reversion to some savage past, it was significantly *modern*. Of course, there had been mass-murders and genocides before but, as Bauman says, the Holocaust put to shame all previous equivalents in its adoption of rational, planned, scientifically informed, expert, efficiently managed, coordinated methods.

It is often asked how this bureaucracy could function when the moral implications were apparently so clear. How could ordinary people be so morally blind? The answer that Bauman gives is that it is the whole *point* of bureaucracy to divorce morality from action, to depersonalize and dehumanize. So, if violence is an adequate solution to a problem, bureaucratic procedures divest it of moral connotations. There is a task to perform and moral or personal scruples simply get in the way.

Bureaucracies also systematically introduce a distance between an act and its consequences. They are complex hierarchies in which any order takes time to trickle through the layers. There is a great distance between intention and accomplishment, with the space between packed with a multitude of little acts. So the bureaucrat who orders extermination does not carry out the act; the man who carries it out did not order it. In much the same way the workers in an arms factory threatened with closure can welcome an order for armaments that will eventually be used to kill civilians. The rationalization so characteristic of modern society therefore removes morality. It splits apart the objectives of our actions from the means that we use to achieve them and makes us concentrate on the latter and ignore the former.

At the beginning of this chapter, I contrasted rationalized action with spontaneous, emotional, spiritual action. The very pervasiveness of rationalization means that action flowing from these other impulses may become squeezed out. Rationalization may produce *disenchantment*. The natural, joyous, playful aspects of life will be overtaken by a ruthless concentration on efficient means to ends. Magic, religion, the unknown are all banished by a rigorous rationalized science. Tolkein's book *The Lord of the Rings* (and the films which are based on it) exemplifies this disenchantment. It is a story of hobbits, elves, dwarves and wizards who inhabit a world of magic, joy, song, immortality and great events. But it is a world that is passing because of the advent of men who have no magic and rely on planning, science and machines.

More sociologically, Norbert Elias argues that the history of European societies is a history of the disciplining of natural impulses.[21] He talks of a process of *civilization* which has lasted from the Middle Ages until the present. What this process did was to impose a series of disciplines – rules – on the conduct of everyday life. In particular, there is increasing regulation of aggression, rudeness, emotion, feeling, natural behaviour and the spontaneous outburst.

One way in which he seeks to illustrate this argument is in the creation of manners. In manners while eating, for example, there were relatively few prohibitions on behaviour at table during the Middle Ages. Treatises on manners written at the time therefore allowed everyone to take food from a common dish and eat with their fingers. It was deemed bad manners to put something one had chewed back into the common pot, or to offer a tasty morsel from one's own mouth to a friend. If swallowing was an impossibility, the recommendation was to throw the offending food on the floor. One should not blow one's nose on the table cloth, nor into the hand which one used for taking food from the common dish. The table cloth was there for wiping one's hands. Very few implements were used and everyone carried their own knife.

By the sixteenth century, forks and spoons for individual use were becoming more common. By the late seventeenth century, soup was no longer eaten directly from the common dish but a spoon was used to serve into individual plates. Even then there was a risk that someone would help themselves to soup with a spoon that had already been in their mouth. It was only towards the end of the eighteenth century in Europe that table manners became recognizably modern in upper-class society, and it was a further hundred years before they became diffused throughout society.

Elias makes similar points about spitting and blowing one's nose. In the Middle Ages it was customary to spit in public. Spitting was considered as much a bodily need as urinating. Gradually, in succeeding centuries the custom became limited. In the sixteenth century it was required that the sputum be trodden under foot. Later it was conventional to use a handkerchief. By the nineteenth century spitting in public was considered a disgusting habit, although it still took a century before it disappeared altogether. Similarly with blowing one's nose. In the Middle Ages, people would blow their noses with their fingers and wipe off the residue on their clothes. It was not until the seventeenth century that handkerchiefs became at all common among the upper classes, but the treatises on manners still found it necessary to warn people against looking at the product or poking a finger up one's nose.

The relatively simple expressions of natural functions or spontaneous activities have therefore become, over several centuries, greatly more controlled by an extensive set of rules. These rules are not merely more extensive, they are also taken for granted; we would simply not think of performing otherwise.

A similar argument is advanced about the evolution of rules governing sporting events. On the face of it, all societies have played sports, but the ancient and medieval versions were fundamentally different from the modern ones. For example, Greek boxing and wrestling were relatively much more violent and less hedged about with rules. It was not at all unusual for participants to be killed, rules were frequently vague and could often not be enforced, and there was no time-limit to bouts, which were only deemed to be over when one contestant gave up. Elias notes that, in pre-industrial England, an early version of football was played. People – any number of people – used to gather on some open ground and kick an inflated pig's bladder around. Rules were rudimentary and games, again, had no start and finish time. The games were frequently excuses for fighting, and large numbers of people could be hurt. There is an obvious contrast between these early sports and the modern ones, which have written rules enforced by referees and backed by international bodies.

In saying that the rational rules of modern society discipline natural, violent or emotional behaviour, it is also important to be clear what Elias is not saying. He is not claiming that these emotions somehow vanish but only that they are channelled and controlled. Football matches are still exciting, but the pleasure in modern times is of a different kind. It is the excitement of being a spectator rather than a participant.

In describing the process of rationalization, I have conjured up a particular image of our social world – organized, efficient, calculating, measuring, controlling, disenchanting. Above all, perhaps, it is an image of an ordered (though not necessarily calm) existence broken only by bureaucratic ineptitude. But rationalization, like so much human activity, is contradictory. It may bring organized and planned genocide, but it can also make sure that food and water are brought to starving populations. It may curb spontaneity, magic and freedom within a web of rules, but it also restrains violence. Furthermore, as I have tried to show in this book, control is difficult to achieve and is constantly undermined. Efficiency through calculation and measurement is an ideal regularly unattained in our daily lives. The world continues to offer enchantment. In sum, modern societies are riven by a tendency to rationalization which is routinely frustrated.

# What can sociology do for you?

The fascination of sociology lies in the fact that its perspective makes us see in a new light the very world in which we have lived all our lives.

Peter Berger

In chapter 2, I described the way in which human organizations create informal cultures that operate largely unconsciously but nonetheless very powerfully. Throughout the rest of the book, I have given other examples applying to social institutions of all sizes – couples, families, local communities and whole societies. Social life is only possible because of background conventions and assumptions – cultures – which only emerge into the light of day when challenged by a contrast with other ways of behaving.

From the sociologist's point of view, probably the most important thing about all of these background assumptions is that they are routinely *unexamined*. The whole point is that they are so interwoven with the conduct of everyday life that they are unnoticed, and they function so well for that reason. In fact, they are so thoroughly accepted that they may well seem *natural*. To revert to an example that I cited earlier in the book, it seems entirely natural, perhaps even biologically determined, to treat children in a particular way – to refrain from seriously beating them, not to sexually abuse them, and not to send them out to work at the age of six. To transgress any of these principles then seems like an offence against nature – yet, in fact, they are not the assumptions of all societies.

In the last chapter I gave an account of rationalization. The whole point of that argument is that the processes of rationalization inform, and underpin, everyday life. We are, however, not aware of them, for that is simply how life is; we do not question it systematically, if at all. It seems to be a wholly natural way of going on. The Wenhastons, therefore, have to organize, calculate and measure throughout their day; there is simply no other way of living. One way of putting this is to say that we are rationalized *personalities*. Rationalization is not something that is *done* to us as unwilling subjects; quite the contrary, we have thoroughly internalized its practices and procedures. In fact, it is this very aspect that has so horrified novelists such as Orwell, Huxley and Kafka. It is not the servitude that is imposed from outside that is truly frightening; that can always be overthrown. But if people *volunteer* to be unfree, the future is much darker. Stanley Milgram conducted a series of experiments designed to investigate obedience to authority.[1] People were recruited by newspaper advertisements to volunteer to take part in psychological experiments on the connection between punishment and learning. These people (let us call them 'teachers') were asked to administer electric shocks to persons sitting behind a glass screen – call these 'subjects'. The subjects had to learn pairs of words. If they made a mistake, an electric shock was administered and, with each successive mistake, the shock was increased in intensity. The teacher was faced with a panel of switches marked from 15 volts up to 450 volts, with 'slight shock' at 15, 'danger – severe shock' at 375, and simply 'XXX' at 450. The atmosphere was scientific and the teacher was accompanied by an experimenter in a white coat whose role was to guide the teacher in the administration of the shocks.

In fact, the whole experimental set-up was a fake. The subject supposed to be learning was an actor. There were no electric shocks. The experimenter, another actor, was there as a figure of authority to give the orders to the teacher. The whole fiction worked though. The actor writhed in pain, banged on the walls, and begged for the experiment to stop. There was no doubt that the teachers *thought* that they were administering electric shocks.

And there is the rub. Almost all the teachers – the *real* targets of the experiment – went all the way up to the full strength of the XXX shocks. People knowingly inflicted pain in obedience to the authority of the experimenter. Milgram concluded that there is a basic assumption of obedience to authority; we have all *internalized* obedience.

The story does, however, have a less depressing ending. Milgram conducted several variations on his initial experiment, bringing it closer to real-life situations. He tried having more than one teacher present, having the subjects physically close to the teacher, and having more than one experimenter, who then disagreed with one another. In each of these variations, far more of the teachers resisted the commands of the experimenter.

To say that basic assumptions are routinely unexamined is not to say that they are *undiscussed*. Actually they may form the staple of everyday conversation. Thus, friends and neighbours may talk to each other about ungrateful or disrespectful children, the peculiarities of other neighbours or the difficulties of persuading husbands to do housework. However, these conversations are really occasions for *confirmation* of the culture of the group. People are looking for support for their view of the world in an exchange of views and anecdotes. They would be both surprised and offended to be contradicted regularly. Generally speaking, we live our lives in a circle of people very like us, and everybody in that circle is liable to share the same background assumptions. In chapter 7, I described a study of the role of gossip in controlling the lives of young people in a London Punjabi community. Gossip is effectively a device for the assertion and maintenance of the background assumptions about the way that a community lives its life.

It is sociology's task to challenge these stories and question basic assumptions, and it has been the purpose of this book to show how that is done. The existence, and also the power, of basic assumptions is often most clearly demonstrated when cultures confront each other. A study by Liebes and Katz shows how this happens.[2] The authors are interested in explaining the global appeal of the television series *Dallas*, which was shown in some ninety countries during the late 1970s and early 1980s. They interviewed people from six different communities with radically different cultures and languages. Four of these came from Israel – Arab citizens, Russian immigrants, Moroccan Jews of long standing and residents of a kibbutz born in Israel. To these were added people from the west coast of the United States (for whom the programme was originally intended) and people from Japan (where the programme failed).

Several groups from each of these communities were shown an episode of *Dallas* and then were asked to retell the episode in their groups (rather than individually). Groups from different communities retold the story in very different ways. Perhaps unsurprisingly, different moral judgements were made of what was going on in the story. But all groups were also very selective in the retelling. They would concentrate on particular characters, often leaving others out altogether; one story line would be emphasized as crucial when there were others; incidents important to one group would be ignored by others. And the point made by Liebes and Katz is that these retellings are not random mistakes. Groups from the same cultures would retell the story in much the same way and in a quite different way from other cultures and would do so for reasons deeply rooted in the culture. Arabs and Moroccan Jews, for instance, picked out features associated with power and relative position in the family and society, concerns related to their culture and perhaps to their position in Israeli society. At a deeper level, the kinds of retellings produced by each community also differ markedly. Americans and Israelis born in that country retold the episode in terms of the characters of the people involved. Arabs and Moroccan Jews essentially retold the story as a series of actions, rather than the backdrop for the unfolding of character. Russians, on the other hand, ignored both action and character and focused on the message they believed the makers of the programme wished to send. As one said:

> The programme is propaganda for the American way of life. They show American characters. The programme deals with the dilemma of life in America. It is actually advertising – or more accurately, propaganda – for the American way of life. They show the average person in an interesting way the ideal he should be striving towards.[3]

Again, Liebes and Katz interpret this selectivity as a product of the culture. Russian Jews, hardly surprisingly, have come to regard their environment with suspicion.

Literally then, basic assumptions dictate how the world is seen and interpreted. In some cases, it impedes seeing anything at all. For the Japanese participants in the study, the cultural distance was so great that they could hardly engage with *Dallas* at all. They found the characters flat and unsubtle, the plots unbelievable and the whole inconsistent with their view of America. The programme made no sense; as one participant commented: 'It is not a possible story.'

Peter Berger provides an example of how cultural confrontation may be used in teaching.[4] He invites us to imagine a lecture given in the 1960s in the southern United States in which the audience is almost entirely white. The lecture is on race. The material may seem familiar to the students – it is part of their everyday lives after all – even if the words used are a little strange. The students live in an environment in which black people occupy an inferior place, and that probably seems entirely natural. The lecturer then moves to a discussion of the caste system of India and suggests that there are similarities between the social structure of India and that of the southern United States. That comparison is revealing, for it implies that the ethnic divisions of the South are very like the caste system of a completely different kind of society. At the best, it will force the students to question the basic assumptions of their everyday lives.

In questioning the basic assumptions and stories of everyday life, sociology is looking beneath the obvious, the taken for granted. Sociology, in adopting a method of systematic doubt, is effectively trying to stand outside the basic assumptions and see them as artifice – as did the Russians in Katz and Liebes's study. Such an enterprise, in turn, is informed by the view that what lies beneath the whirlpool of everyday life is a pattern, a structure, that explains the phenomena we experience.[5] All this is not to claim that sociology's findings are always surprising. As I argued earlier in the book, the subject's inquiries can often confirm what people already know. It does imply, however, that sociology can be provocative, undermining and upsetting, as any questioning of basic assumptions is likely to be. And this, I would claim, makes sociology a moral enterprise. I do not mean by this that sociology and sociologists take a particular moral stance on society. Sociologists as individuals may have political and social values, but those values should not influence the work that they do. I mean, rather, that the task of questioning basic assumptions is in itself a moral task. Only in that way can we hope to change our lives.

# Notes

## PREFACE

1   P. Berger, *Invitation to Sociology*. Harmondsworth: Penguin, 1963.

## CHAPTER 1   THE REALITY OF EVERYDAY LIFE

1   Indeed, it is precisely to overcome such strangeness that most people have rituals that they go through in order to mark out the provinces and keep them separate. See C. E. Nippert-Eng, 'Transitional acts as rituals', in T. Bennett and D. Watson (eds), *Understanding Everyday Life*. Oxford: Blackwell, 2002.
2   For a further discussion of the way in which everyday life gives security, see A. Giddens, *The Constitution of Society*. Cambridge: Polity, 1984. Silverstone shows the way in which television, so often thought of as a disruptive influence, is actually a part of the soothing routine of everyday life (R. Silverstone, *Television and Everyday Life*. London: Routledge, 1994).
3   And it is becoming *more* differentiated, as I will be showing in future chapters.
4   See R. Berthoud and J. Gershuny (eds), *Seven Years in the Lives of British Families*. Bristol: Policy Press, 2000.

## CHAPTER 2   WHO DO WE THINK WE ARE?

1   H. Becker, *Outsiders*. New York: Free Press, 1966.
2   Ibid., p. 48.
3   For further discussion of this point, see R. Jenkins, *Social Identity*. London: Routledge, 1996, chapter 8.

4    As the film *The Crying Game* shows. One of the central characters appears in the earlier parts of the film to be a woman but turns out to be biologically male. The point is that, not only do the characters in the film believe that he is a woman, but so also does the audience.

5    See H. Garfinkel, Studies in *Ethnomethodology*. Englewood Cliffs, NJ: Prentice-Hall, 1967. Garfinkel's style does not make it easy for the reader. For an account that is more comprehensible, see J. Heritage, *Garfinkel and Ethnomethodology*. Cambridge: Polity, 1984.

6    There is a large literature on this point. For example, see C. MacCormack and M. Strathern (eds), *Nature, Culture and Gender*. Cambridge: Cambridge University Press, 1980.

7    R. Jackall, *Moral Mazes*. New York: Oxford University Press, 1988.

8    B. Anderson, *Imagined Communities*. London: Verso, 1991.

9    For a further discussion, see N. Abercrombie and B. Longhurst, *Audiences*. London: Sage, 1998, chapter 4.

10    See J. Stacey, *Stargazing: Hollywood Cinema and Female Spectatorship*. London: Routledge, 1994.

11    J. Hermes, *Reading Women's Magazines*. Cambridge: Polity, 1995.

12    K. J. Fox, 'Real punks and pretenders: the social organization of a counterculture'. *Journal of Contemporary Ethnography*, 16, 4, 1987.

13    The same phenomenon may be observed in other social settings. For example, a study of hot-rod enthusiasts in the United States noted that the social structure of those interested in hot-rod cars could be represented as a set of concentric circles (see H. F. Moorhouse, *Driving Ambitions: An Analysis of the American Hot-Rod Enthusiasm*. Manchester: Manchester University Press, 1991). At the centre is the core, which is made up of professionals and amateurs. The former make their living from the enthusiasm while the latter are greatly involved and operate as a kind of conscience regulating the more commercial activities of the professionals. Around the core is a layer of the interested public of those who have a part-time interest at most, and beyond them the general public. The outer rings comprise those who are deemed by those in the inner rings to be less authentic, interested only in buying the commercial paraphernalia of the sport but not *really* involved.

14    See B. J. Longhurst, *Popular Music and Society*. Cambridge: Polity, 1995.

15    S. Frith and H. Horne, *Art into Pop*. London: Routledge, 1987.

16    M. Gillespie, *Television, Ethnicity and Cultural Change*. London: Routledge, 1995.

17    R. Wallis, *The Elementary Forms of the New Religious Life*. London: Routledge, 1984.

18    S. S. Larsen, 'The two sides of the house: identity and social organization in Kilbroney, Northern Ireland', in A. P. Cohen (ed.), *Belonging: Identity and Social Organization in British Rural Cultures*. Manchester: Manchester University Press, 1982.

19    D. Southerton, 'Boundaries of "us" and "them": class, mobility and identification in a new town'. *Sociology*, 36, 1, 2002.

20    For further reading on globalization, see M. Albrow, *The Global Age*. Cambridge: Polity, 1996.

21   See N. Abercrombie, A. Warde et al., *Contemporary British Society*. 3rd edn, Cambridge: Polity, 2000, p. 385. A similar argument may be advanced about football. Thus, P. McGovern ('Globalization or internationalization? Foreign footballers in the English league, 1946–95'. *Sociology*, 36, 1, 2002) suggests that, although football is so often described as globalized, actually English clubs tend to draw on those overseas sources that most resemble England.

22   For an argument along these lines, see M. Billig, *Banal Nationalism*. London: Sage, 1995.

23   F. Bechhofer et al., 'Constructing national identity: arts and landed elites in Scotland'. *Sociology*, 33, 3, 1999; repr. in N. Abercrombie and A. Warde, *The Contemporary British Society Reader*. Cambridge: Polity, 2001.

24   K. Roberts, 'Same activities, different meanings: British youth cultures in the 1990s'. *Leisure Studies*, 16, 1997; repr. in N. Abercrombie and A. Warde, *The Contemporary British Society Reader*.

25   A. Giddens, *Modernity and Self-Identity*. Cambridge: Polity, 1991.

## CHAPTER 3   WHO DO WE LOVE?

1   A rather sour view of the pursuit of intimacy as a goal of personal relationships is provided by R. Sennett, *The Fall of Public Man*. London: Faber & Faber, 1977. As he says:

> The reigning belief today is that closeness between persons is a moral good. The reigning aspiration today is to develop individual personality through experiences of closeness and warmth with others. The reigning myth today is that the evils of society can all be understood as evils of impersonality, alienation, and coldness. The sum of these three is an ideology of intimacy: social relationships of all kinds are real, believable, and authentic the closer they approach the inner psychological concerns of each person. (p. 259)

2   P. Burke, *The Art of Conversation*. Cambridge: Polity, 1993.

3   A. Giddens, *The Transformation of Intimacy*. Cambridge: Polity, 1992.

4   J. Duncombe and D. Marsden, 'Can men love? "Reading", "staging" and "resisting" the romance', in L. Pearce and J. Stacey (eds), *Romance Revisited*. New York: New York University Press, 1995, p. 245.

5   S. Hite, *The New Hite Report: Women and Love: A Cultural Revolution in Progress*. London: Viking/Penguin, 1987.

6   M. Mac an Ghaill, *The Making of Men*. Buckingham: Open University Press, 1994.

7   P. Redman, 'Love is in the air: romance and the everyday', in T. Bennett and D. Watson (eds), *Understanding Everyday Life*. Oxford: Blackwell, 2002, p. 63.

8   Ibid., p. 64.

9   J. Giles, 'You meet 'em and that's it: working class women's refusal of

romance between the wars in Britain', in L. Pearce and J. Stacey (eds), *Romance Revisited*.

10  P. Mansfield and J. Collard, *The Beginning of the Rest of your Life?*. Basingstoke: Macmillan, 1988.

11  Prinz believes that all European countries are undergoing a demographic revolution in which cohabitation is replacing marriage. Different countries are at different stages. Great Britain is fairly advanced and only Norway and Sweden are further ahead (C. Prinz, *Cohabiting, Married or Single*. Aldershot: Avebury, 1995). Laurie and Gershuny, on the other hand, argue that cohabiting unions last only a short time before either dissolving or being turned into marriage (H. Laurie and J. Gershuny, 'Patterns of household and family formation', in R. Berthoud and J. Gershuny (eds), *Seven Years in the Lives of British Families*. Bristol: Policy Press, 2000).

12  See S. McRae, 'Introduction: family and household change in Britain', in S. McRae (ed.), *Changing Britain: Families and Households in the 1990s*. Oxford: Oxford University Press, 1999.

13  F. McAllister with L. Clarke, *Choosing Childlessness*. London: Family Policy Studies Centre, 1998.

14  R. Hall, P. E. Ogden and C. Hill, 'Living alone: evidence from England and Wales and France for the last two decades', in S. McRae (ed.), *Changing Britain: Families and Households in the 1990s*.

15  See, for example, E. Bott, *Family and Social Network*. London: Tavistock, 1957; M. Young and P. Willmott, *Family and Kinship in East London*. London: Routledge, 1957; J. H. Goldthorpe, D. Lockwood, F. Bechhofer and J. Platt, *The Affluent Worker in the Class Structure*. Cambridge: Cambridge University Press, 1969; M. Young and P. Willmott, *The Symmetrical Family*. London: Routledge, 1973.

16  J. Gershuny, 'Change in the domestic division of labour in the UK, 1975–1987: dependent labour versus adaptive partnership', in N. Abercrombie and A. Warde (eds), *Social Change in Contemporary Britain*. Cambridge: Polity, 1992; H. Laurie and J. Gershuny, 'Patterns of household and family formation', in R. Berthoud and J. Gershuny (eds), *Seven Years in the Lives of British Families*.

17  S. Edgell, *Middle Class Couples*. London: Allen & Unwin, 1980.

18  J. Pahl, *Money and Marriage*. London: Macmillan, 1989.

19  N. Charles and N. Kerr, *Women, Food and Families*. Manchester: Manchester University Press, 1988.

20  D. Morley, *Family Television: Cultural Power and Domestic Leisure*. London: Comedia, 1986.

21  For a recent account, see C. Heywood, *A History of Childhood*. Cambridge: Polity, 2001.

22  K. Grahame, *The Wind in the Willows*. London: Methuen, 1951, p. 107.

23  An interesting variety of viewpoints on the significance of 'home' in contemporary society is provided in G. Allan and G. Crow (eds), *Home and Family*. Basingstoke: Macmillan, 1989.

24  P. Saunders, *A Nation of Home Owners*. London: Allen & Unwin, 1990, pp. 299–300.

25   For a cautionary note, see G. Allan and G. Crow, 'Privatization, home-centredness and leisure'. *Leisure Studies*, 10, 1, 1991.

26   M. Franklin, 'Working class privatism: an historical case study of Bedminster, Bristol'. *Society and Space*, 1989.

27   R. D. Putnam, *Bowling Alone: The Collapse and Revival of American Community*. New York: Simon & Schuster, 2000.

28   C. Phillipson, M. Bernard, J. Phillips and J. Ogg, 'Older people's experiences of community life in patterns of neighbouring in three urban communities'. *Sociological Review*, 37, 1999.

29   G. Allan, *A Sociology of Friendship and Kinship*. London: Allen & Unwin, 1979.

30   A. Giddens, *Modernity and Self-Identity*. Cambridge: Polity, 1991.

31   R. Inglehart, *Culture Shift in Advanced Industrial Society*. Princeton, NJ: Princeton University Press, 1990.

32   R. Hall, P. E. Ogden and C. Hill, 'Living alone: evidence from England and Wales and France for the last two decades', in S. McRae (ed.), *Changing Britain*.

## CHAPTER 4   WHO DO WE TALK TO?

1   Short and accessible introductions to the work of Emile Durkheim are: A. Giddens, *Durkheim*. Glasgow: Collins, 1978; and F. Parkin, *Durkheim*. Oxford: Oxford University Press, 1992.

2   E. Durkheim, *Suicide*. London: Routledge & Kegan Paul, 1952 (original French edition 1897).

3   P. Brierley, *The Tide is Running Out*. London: Christian Research, 2000.

4   N. Abercrombie, A. Warde et al., *Contemporary British Society*. 3rd edn, Cambridge: Polity, 2000, pp. 323–4.

5   A. Greeley, 'Religion in Britain, Ireland and the USA', in R. Jowell, L. Brook, G. Prior and B. Taylor (eds), *British Social Attitudes 9*. Aldershot: Dartmouth, 1992.

6   F. McGlone, A. Park and C. Roberts, 'Relative values: kinship and friendship', in R. Jowell, J. Curtice, A. Park, L. Brook and K. Thomson (eds), *British Social Attitudes 13*. Aldershot: Dartmouth, 1996; F. McGlone, A. Park and K. Smith, *Families and Kinship*. London: Family Policy Studies Centre, 1998; F. McGlone, A. Park and C. Roberts, 'Kinship and friendship: attitudes and behaviour in Britain, 1986–1995', in S. McRae (ed.), *Changing Britain: Families and Households in the 1990s*. Oxford: Oxford University Press, 1999. Unlike many of the earlier studies, this set of investigations is founded on a large sample survey and is not based in one locality.

7   Of course, the way that people *think* about distance is actually highly variable, so simple geographical proximity may be rather misleading. For some, a separation from relatives of one hour's journey is an unthinkable divide while, for others, a journey of two or three hours is perfectly possible.

8   J. Bornat, B. Dimmock, B. Jones and S. Peace, 'The impact of family change

on older people: the case of stepfamilies', in S. McRae (ed.), *Changing Britain*.

9   See, for example, R. Frankenburg, *Communities in Britain*. Harmondsworth: Penguin, 1966.

10   The classical study is M. Young and P. Willmott, *Family and Kinship in East London*. London: Routledge, 1957.

11   Young and Willmott's *Family and Kinship in East London* also contained a study of a suburban council estate which they called Greenleigh.

12   P. Willmott and M. Young, *Family and Class in a London Suburb*. London: Routledge & Kegan Paul, 1960.

13   G. Crow, G. Allan and M. Summers, 'Neither busybodies nor nobodies: managing proximity and distance in neighbourly relations'. *Sociology*, 36, 1, 2002.

14   Ibid., p. 139.

15   P. A. Hall, 'Social capital in Britain'. *British Journal of Political Science*, 29, 1999, pp. 417–61.

16   *Social Trends*, 2000.

17   J. Bishop and P. Hoggett, *Organizing around Enthusiasms*. London: Comedia, 1986.

18   L. Barber, *Mostly Men*. Harmondsworth: Penguin, 1991.

19   C. Bacon-Smith, *Enterprising Women: Television Fandom and the Creation of Popular Myth*. Philadelphia: University of Pennsylvania Press, 1992; and H. Jenkins, *Textual Poachers: Television Fans and Participatory Culture*. London: Routledge, 1992. For a sociological account of fandom, see N. Abercrombie and B. Longhurst, *Audiences*. London: Sage, 1998.

20   See note 6 for details of the study.

21   C. Phillipson, M. Bernard, J. Phillips and J. Ogg, 'The family and community life of old people'. *Ageing and Society*, 18, 1998.

22   R. D. Putnam, *Bowling Alone: The Collapse and Revival of American Community*. New York: Simon & Schuster, 2000.

23   A similar conclusion was reached in the previous chapter in the discussion of individualism. Later generations are more interested in individual self-expression than in community relations.

## CHAPTER 5   IS WORK A CURSE?

1   The classical statement of this argument can be found in E. P. Thompson, 'Time, work-discipline, and industrial capitalism'. *Past and Present*, 38, 1967. An abridged version may be found reprinted in A. Giddens and D. Held (eds), *Classes, Power, and Conflict*. Berkeley and Los Angeles: University of California Press, 1982.

2   B. Martin and S. Mason, 'Some current trends in leisure: taking account of time'. *Leisure Studies*, 13, 2, 1994.

3   M. Taylor, 'Work, non-work and job mobility', in R. Berthoud and J. Gershuny (eds), *Seven Years in the Lives of British Families*. Bristol: Policy Press, 2000.

 4  Quoted in A. Sinfield, *What Unemployment Means*. Oxford: Martin
    Robertson, 1981, p. 41.
 5  C. Dickens, *Little Dorrit*. Oxford: Oxford University Press, 1981, p. 104
    (orig. pubn 1857).
 6  The classical account is to be found in M. Weber, *Economy and Society*.
    New York: Free Press, 1968, chapter 11.
 7  R. Jackall, *Moral Mazes*. New York: Oxford University Press, 1988.
 8  Ibid., p. 64.
 9  Ibid., p. 38.
10  N. Abercrombie, A. Warde et al., *Contemporary British Society*. Cambridge:
    Polity, 2000, p. 95.
11  S. Westwood, *All Day Every Day*. London: Pluto, 1984.
12  L. Taylor and P. Walton, 'Industrial sabotage: motives and meanings', in
    S. Cohen (ed.), *Images of Deviance*. Harmondsworth: Penguin, 1971.
13  N. Abercrombie, A. Warde et al., *Contemporary British Society*, p. 58.
14  See A. Warde, *Eating Out*. Cambridge: Cambridge University Press, 2000.
15  Y. Gabriel, *Working Lives in Catering*. London: Routledge, 1988, p. 58.
16  M. Taylor, 'Work, non-work, jobs and job mobility'.
17  But for a contrary view, see R. Taylor (*Britain's World of Work – Myths
    and Realities*. Swindon: ESRC, 2002), who argues that there are more
    permanent jobs and job tenure is lengthening.
18  See A. Phizacklea and C. Wolfowitz, *Homeworking Women*. London: Sage,
    1995.
19  R. Taylor, *Britain's World of Work*.
20  F. Green, 'It's been a hard day's night: the concentration and intensification
    of work in late twentieth century Britain'. *British Journal of Industrial Rela-
    tions*, 39, 2001, pp. 53–80.
21  R. Taylor, *Britain's World of Work*.
22  For an account, see S. Harkness, 'Working 9 to 5?', in P. Gregg and
    J. Wadsworth, *The State of Working Britain*. Manchester: Manchester
    University Press, 1999.
23  Managers also said that they worked long hours because they found the job
    interesting, though this factor was not as significant as the requirements of
    the job.
24  D. Wainwright and M. Calnan, *Work Stress*. Buckingham: Open University
    Press, 2002.
25  A. Hochschild, *The Time Bind*. New York: Metropolitan Books, 1997.
26  H. Bradley, M. Erickson, C. Stephenson and S. Williams, *Myths at Work*.
    Cambridge: Polity, 2000, p. 180.
27  Ibid., p. 136.

## CHAPTER 6   DOES INEQUALITY MATTER?

 1  *The Guardian*, 10 May 2002.
 2  N. Abercrombie, A. Warde et al., *Contemporary British Society*. 3rd edn,
    Cambridge: Polity, 2000, p. 491.

3   Ibid., p. 258.
4   Ibid., p. 249.
5   K. Grint, *The Sociology of Work*. Cambridge: Polity, 1998.
6   J. Hills, *Joseph Rowntree Inquiry into Income and Wealth*. York: Joseph Rowntree, 1995. See also N. Abercrombie, A. Warde et al., *Contemporary British Society*, chapter 5.2. If state benefits are excluded from the calculation, the ratio is 30 to 1.
7   S. P. Jenkins, 'Dynamics of household incomes', in R. Berthoud and J. Gershuny (eds), *Seven Years in the Lives of British Families*. Bristol: Policy Press, 2000.
8   P. Gregg and J. Wadsworth, 'More work in fewer households', in J. Hills (ed.), *New Inequalities*. Cambridge: Cambridge University Press, 1996.
9   These data and those on poverty from N. Abercrombie, A. Warde et al., *Contemporary British Society*, chapter 5.2.
10  S. P. Jenkins, 'Dynamics of household incomes'.
11  J. Stewart, 'Poverty and social security', Department of Applied Social Science, University of Lancaster, 1997.
12  R. Cohen, J. Coxell, G. Craig and A. Sadiq-Sangster, *Hardship Britain*. London: Child Poverty Action Group, 1992, p. 89.
13  Ibid., p. 72.
14  H. Graham, 'The challenge of health inequalities', in H. Graham (ed.), *Understanding Health Inequalities*. Buckingham: Open University Press, 2000.
15  R. G. Wilkinson, *Unhealthy Societies*. London: Routledge, 1996.
16  See chapter 2 for a discussion of the way in which boundaries between social groups are maintained.
17  For further discussion of the position of the upper class, see J. Scott, *The Upper Classes*. London: Macmillan, 1982; and his *Who Rules Britain*. Cambridge: Polity, 1991.
18  A more detailed guide to material on the middle class can be found in N. Abercrombie, A. Warde et al., *Contemporary British Society*, chapter 6.4.
19  Ibid., p. 152. The traditional distinction between manual and non-manual work is becoming increasingly difficult to sustain. The distinction between working as a care assistant, as a photocopying clerk, and as a burger flipper is muddy.
20  Ibid., chapter 6.2.
21  G. Marshall, D. Rose, H. Newby and C. Vogler, *Social Class in Modern Britain*. London: Unwin Hyman, 1988.
22  B. Skeggs, *Formations of Class and Gender*. London: Sage, 1997.
23  Ibid., p. 75.
24  Ibid., p. 3.
25  And, at the risk of confusion, I will be referring to this composite as the service class. This has been a very short discussion of social class in Britain. Recent lengthier treatments are: J. Westergaard, *Who Gets What?*. Cambridge: Polity, 1995; M. Savage, *Class Analysis and Social Transformation*. Buckingham: Open University Press, 2000; and K. Roberts, *Class in Modern*

*Britain*. Basingstoke: Palgrave, 2001. For a rather different approach, see P. Saunders, *Social Class and Stratification*. London: Routledge, 1990.

26  There is a more detailed sociological version of this argument. See the debate between Moore and Tumin which is reprinted in section 9 of J. Scott (ed.), *Class: Critical Concepts*, vol. 3. London: Routledge, 1996.

27  Still an important study, though now old, is: J. Goldthorpe with C. Llewellyn and C. Payne, *Social Mobility and Class Structure in Modern Britain*. Oxford: Oxford University Press, 1980. See also G. Marshall, A. Swift and S. Roberts, *Against the Odds?*. Oxford: Oxford University Press, 1997; and, for a dissenting view, P. Saunders, *Unequal but Fair?*. London: Institute for Economic Affairs, 1996. My account here is dependent on Marshall, Swift and Roberts's book and on G. Marshall and A. Swift, 'Social class and social justice'. *British Journal of Sociology*, 44, 2, 1993. See also P. Saunders, 'Might Britain be a meritocracy?'. *Sociology*, 29, 1, 1995.

## CHAPTER 7   WHY DON'T THINGS FALL APART?

1  All in *Sunday Express*, 25 August 2002.

2  *Sunday Mirror*, 25 August 2002.

3  See K. Thompson, *Moral Panics*. London: Routledge, 1998.

4  The classical account of the mechanisms of moral panics of this kind is S. Cohen, *Folk Devils and Moral Panics: The Creation of Mods and Rockers*. Oxford: Martin Robertson, 1980. Cohen (whose book was first published in 1972) argues that, at certain times of social stress, societies get into moral panics about a particular social issue or group, during which a great deal of attention is focused. His study concentrated on the conflicts in southern seaside towns between mods and rockers but could apply to many situations, including travellers and refugees. The media have a major role in amplifying the panic, and because of this media attention, the agencies of social control – the government, the police, the courts – are driven to devise new policies for the control of the groups concerned. This gives a further turn to the screw in that government action or police attention that results in arrests and convictions is reported on television and in the press, further fuelling the sense of moral panic.

5  The original account of moral entrepreneurship can be found in H. Becker, *Outsiders*. New York: Free Press, 1966. Becker is interested in how rules are made rather than why people break them. He shows how powerful individuals engage in moral crusades which create a climate in which new rules are made and legislation introduced.

6  N. Abercrombie, A. Warde et al., *Contemporary British Society*. 3rd edn, Cambridge: Polity, 2000, p. 535. These are expressed at constant prices.

7  *The Guardian*, 27 August 2002.

8  S. Cohen, *Visions of Social Control*. Cambridge: Polity, 1985.

9  *The Guardian*, 27 August 2002.

10  Just as in Orwell's *1984*.

11  M. Gillespie, *Television, Ethnicity and Cultural Change*. London:

Routledge, 1995. The film *Bend it Like Beckham* also illustrates the power of gossip in a relatively closed community.

12    G. Sykes, *The Society of Captives*. Princeton, NJ: Princeton University Press, 1958.

13    H. Garfinkel, *Studies in Ethnomethodology*. Englewood Cliffs, NJ: Prentice-Hall, 1967.

14    P. Marsh, E. Rosser and R. Harre, *The Rules of Disorder*. London: Routledge, 1978.

15    M. Abrams, D. Gerard and N. Timms (eds), *Values and Social Change in Britain*. Basingstoke: Macmillan, 1985.

16    T. Lane and K. Roberts, *Strike at Pilkingtons*. London: Fontana, 1971.

17    R. Titmuss, *The Gift Relationship*. London: Allen & Unwin, 1970.

18    J. Finch and J. Mason, *Negotiating Family Responsibilities*. London: Routledge, 1993.

19    Ibid., p. 150.

20    The early sociologists were particularly interesting in this respect. Durkheim (1858–1917), for example, argued that there had to be a moral basis, even for contemporary society which stressed the apparently untrammelled rights of the individual. He wrote: 'Thus altruism is not destined to become . . . a sort of agreeable ornament to social life, but it will forever be its fundamental basis. How can we ever really dispense with it? Men cannot live together without acknowledging, and, consequently, making mutual sacrifices, without tying themselves to one another with strong, durable bonds. Every society is a moral society' (*The Division of Labour in Society*. New York: Free Press, 1964).

21    R. Putnam (*Bowling Alone: The Collapse and Revival of American Community*. New York: Simon & Schuster, 2000) offers an interesting discussion of trust in the contemporary United States.

## CHAPTER 8   HAS THE MAGIC GONE?

1    I owe this example to G. Ritzer, *The McDonaldization of Society*. Newbury Park, CA: Pine Forge Press, 1993.

2    The sociological use of the term originates with Max Weber. See particularly his *The Protestant Ethic and the Spirit of Capitalism*. London: Allen & Unwin, 1930. For an extension of his ideas, and a lively read, see G. Ritzer, *The McDonaldization of Society*.

3    Weber made a distinction between formal and substantive rationality to capture the idea that one can adopt perfectly rational means to achieve objectives that appear profoundly irrational. A discussion of the Holocaust later on will illustrate this point.

4    E. P. Thompson, 'Time, work-discipline, and industrial capitalism', in A. Giddens and D. Held (eds), *Classes, Power, and Conflict*. Berkeley: University of California Press, 1982. For a slightly different view, see N. Thrift, 'The making of a capitalist time-consciousness', in J. Hassard (ed.), *The Sociology of Time*. Basingstoke: Macmillan, 1990.

5    Ibid., p. 122.

6   See N. Abercrombie, 'Getting and spending'. *Cultural Values*, 4, 3, 2000.

7   The conventional account is that it is the economic system of capitalism that produces commodification. My interest here is in commodification as measurement in the context of rationalization, and I have accordingly not devoted space to an account of the relationship of commodification to the capitalist mode of production. See R. Lane, *The Market Experience*. Cambridge: Cambridge University Press, 1991; D. Slater and F. Tonkiss, *Market Society*. Cambridge: Polity, 2001.

8   A. R. Hochschild, *The Managed Heart*. Berkeley: University of California Press, 1983.

9   Ibid., p. 4.

10  Ibid., p. 105.

11  Ibid., p. 104.

12  Ibid., p. 109.

13  Ibid., p. 127.

14  A. Smith, *The Wealth of Nations*. London: Methuen, 1950 (orig. pubd 1776).

15  C. Dandekar, *Surveillance, Power and Modernity*. Cambridge: Polity, 1990.

16  H. Beynon, *Working for Ford*. Harmondsworth: Penguin, 1984, p. 129.

17  M. Foucault, *Discipline and Punish*. London: Allen Lane, 1977.

18  Ibid., pp. 6–7.

19  Z. Bauman, *Modernity and the Holocaust*. Cambridge: Polity, 1989.

20  H. L. Feingold, 'How unique is the Holocaust?', in A. Grobman and D. Landes (eds), *Genocide: Critical Issues of the Holocaust*. Los Angeles: Simon Wiesenthal Center, pp. 399–400; quoted in Z. Bauman, *Modernity and the Holocaust*, p. 8.

21  N. Elias, *The Civilizing Process*, vol. 1: *The History of Manners*. Oxford: Blackwell, 1978; N. Elias and E. Dunning, *Quest for Excitement*. Oxford: Blackwell, 1986.

## CHAPTER 9    WHAT CAN SOCIOLOGY DO FOR YOU?

1   S. Milgram, *Obedience to Authority*. London: Tavistock, 1974.

2   T. Liebes and E. Katz, *The Export of Meaning*. Oxford: Oxford University Press, 1993.

3   Ibid., p. 76.

4   P. Berger, *Invitation to Sociology*. Harmondsworth: Penguin, 1966.

5   For a more detailed account of this point, see the still current R. Keat and J. Urry, *Social Theory as Science*. London: Routledge, 1975.

# Index

*About a Boy* (film) 20
abuse, child 99
action: divorced from morality
  115–17; rational 107
activities: identity and 20
adolescents *see* young people
adulthood: marriage as validation of
  27
aesthetic judgements: difficulty of
  109
age: coming of age ceremonies 18;
  post-materialist hypothesis and
  36; social networks and 51;
  social situation and 19–20;
  *see also* old people; young
  people
airlines: emotional labour 110–11
altruism 101–2
*American Beauty* (film) 45
anti-leisure 109
anxiety, social 89–92
appearance: conformity of 11;
  identity and 11
aristocracy *see* upper class
art schools: influence on rock music
  14
associations, social 47–50

assumptions, basic: examination of
  3–5, 120–4
Austen, Jane: personal relationships
  in 23
authenticity: identity and 5, 9,
  13–14, 15
authority: obedience to 121–2
autonomy: emphasis on 35

Bauman, Zygmunt: Holocaust
  115–16
beauty 73
Becker, Howard: identity studies 7–8,
  11, 18
behavioural characteristics:
  relationship with health 78
beliefs, moral *see* moral beliefs
belonging: identity and 8, 10–16;
  strategies of 11–15
Berger, Peter: cultural confrontation
  123
births: outside marriage 28
black people: marriage with white
  15; in prison 92; segregation
  80
blood tranfusion service 101–2
body maintenance 106–7

boundaries: crossing 15, 18; social
    class 81, 85; social groups 15–16
bureaucracy: morality and 116–17;
    organization 58–63
bureaucratic work systems 65, 66

calculation 106–7, 107–11
capital, social 49, 50; decline in
    53–4; social networks as 41; in
    United States 52, 53
care and support: family 102–3; of
    old people 39, 52, 102; in wider
    family 43
caste system 79–80
catering industry 64–5
change, social: identity and 18–21;
    moral panics and 91
child abuse 99
childhood: conceptions of 30–1
childlessness 28
children: born outside marriage 28;
    discipline of 94; mother–child tie
    42–3, 51; in poverty 76–7;
    primary socialization 99; treatment
    of 120
cities: community in 44–5
citizenship: social exclusion 78–9
civic participation see voluntary
    organizations
civil inattention 24
civilization: process of 117–19
class, social: described 80–5; mobility
    86–7; relationship with health 78;
    see also middle class; underclass;
    upper class; working class
clock-orientated societies 108
clubs 48–9
coercion 92–4; limitations of 94–8
cohabitation 27
coming of age ceremonies 18
commitment: identity and 13–14;
    moral 104
commodification 109–11
commonsense: of everyday life 3–5
communication: non-verbal 12; see
    also conversation; language
communities, imagined 13

communities, local: sense of
    belonging 10–11; social
    relationships in 43–7
community programmes: for
    offenders 93–4
commuting 53
companies, small: employment in
    67
computers 65
condition: inequality of 74–9
conduct, moral: connection with
    moral beliefs 100
conformity: of appearance 11
control: efficiency and 114–15; at
    work 61–3; see also coercion
conventions: fan clubs 49
conversation: as art form 23–4; on
    television 33
conversion 13–14; religious 15–16
countryside: community in 44
crime 91–2
criminal justice system: coercion and
    92–4, 95–6
culture: class differences 83;
    confirmation of 122; confrontation
    of 122–3; creation and
    maintenance of 7–8, 97–8; of
    groups 15; informal work 60–1,
    62–3; sense of belonging 11–12;
    youth 11, 13–14, 19–20

Dallas (television series) 122–3
day-dreams: identity and 13; of
    leisure 55
death rates: relationship to income
    78
deprivation 78–9
deviancy: control of 93
Dickens, Charles: bureaucracy 58
difference: compared to inequality
    72–3; identity as 8, 16–21; see also
    diversity
discussions: basic assumptions 122
disenchantment 117
diversity: equality and 72–3; market
    65; of society 19–20; see also
    difference

divorce: increase in rate of 28; remarriage and 29; wider family and 43

DIY 32

dress codes 11

dual burden hypothesis 29–30

Durkheim, Emile: social order 39

education: social class and 86, 87

efficiency 106–7, 111–15

elderly see old people

Elias, Norbert: process of civilization 117–19

email 53

emotion: commodification of 110–11

emotional suffering 70

employment see unemployment; work

enthusiasms: social relationships and 48–9

equality: domestic 29–30; intimacy dependent on 24; see also inequality

equals: secondary socialization 99

estates system 80

ethnic minorities: communities 50; inequality 74; in United States 123; see also black people

everyday life: order in 96–7; reality of 1–5

exchange 101–4; gift 102, 104; indirect 103

exclusion, social 78–9

extended families see families, wider

Faking It (television programme) 12

families: as building blocks of society 38–9; diversity of 19; obligation in 102–4; step-families 43; see also privatism, family

families, wider 40–1; described 41–3

fan clubs 48–50

fantasy 13

fanzines 49

flexible work systems 65–7, 68

folk devils 90–1

football 118, 119

football crowds: social order in 97–8

force: limitations of 95

Fordism 65, 66

Forster, E. M.: 'Machine Stops, The' 35, 38

Foucault, Michel: punishment and surveillance 114–15

fragmentation 19–20, 35

friends 40–1; close 34, 46; as distinct from neighbours 46; intimacy and 33–4; upper class 81; in United States 53

Garfinkel, Harold: social order 96, 99

gender: changing 10; friends and 34; inequality 74; sense of belonging 11; stereotypes of 10; at work 82; see also masculinity; men; women; work, women's

generational change: social relationships and 53

Giddens, Tony: reflexivity 20, 35

gift exchanges 102, 104

globalization 17

Goffman, Erving 24

gossip 15, 94, 122

government policies: coercion 92–4; moral panics 91; unemployment 5

Grahame, Kenneth: Wind in the Willows, The 31

Greece: life expectancy 78

Groundhog Day (film) 2

groups, social: basic assumptions of 122–3; boundaries 15–16; degrees of commitment to 13–14; hierarchy of prestige 4–5; identity and 7–8; sense of belonging 10–11

health: relationship with income 78; social relationships and 54; stress and 70; see also mental health service

health scares 70, 89

hierarchies: in bureaucracy 59; of prestige 4–5, 13–14; of social groups 73

Hitchcock, Alfred 96

hobbies 48–9

Hochschild, Arlie: commodification of human emotion 110–11
Holocaust 115–16
home: ideals of 31–2; working at 67
home ownership 32
honour 80
house, moving: effect on wider family relationships 42; social relationships and 45
households: diversity of 19, 35; single 28, 36; without paid work 57, 76
housework 2, 29–30
housing, quality of: health and 78

identity 6–21; belonging and 10–16; change in 9–10; creation and maintenance of 7–8; as difference 16–21; encapsulated 15–16; malleability of 8, 9, 18–21; moral 103–4; primary 10; reconstruction of 35; self-construction of 20; social construction of 8–10, 20–1; surveillance and 115
illness: stress as 70
imagination: identity and 12–13
imagined communities 13
impersonality: in bureaucracy 59
incentives 85–6
income: inequality in 74–6, 88; relationship with health 78
income tax 75
individualization: young people's biographies 19
individuals: emphasis on 35; inequality of 73
industrialization: effect on families 41–2
inequality 72–88; of condition 74–9; of opportunity 85–8; systems of 79–85
infancy: primary socialization 99
informal practices: work 60–1, 62–3
information: everyday life and 4
inheritance: of opportunity 86
inner cities: community in 44–5
interdependence 101–4

internalization: of common values 98–9; of rationalization 121
intimacy: partnership and 27–9; as private relationship 29–33; risks of 24; romance and 22–7

Katz, E.: cultural confrontation 122–3

labour: emotional 110–11; forced 79
labour, division of 111–14; in bureaucracy 59; domestic 2, 29–30
language: identity and 7, 11–12; nationalist 17–18
learning: identity 8
leisure 55; as distinct from paid work 56; home-based 32–3, 53; time 56–7; time management in 108–9
leisure associations 47–50
Liebes, T.: cultural confrontation 122–3
life-changing events 2–3
life expectancy: inequalities in 78
lifestyle: identity and 20–1; single households 28
living alone see single households
living standards: health and 78
local see communities, local
love, romantic 25, 26–7; see also intimacy

magic: banished by science 117
managers: informal cultures 60–1
Manilow, Barry: fan club 48–9
manners: creation of 117–18
manufacturing: shift to service sector 63–5
marihuana users: study 7, 8, 18
marriage: changes in 27–9; late 27–8; mixed 15, 18; romance and 26–7; upper-class 81; women's dissatisfaction with 25
masculinity 9; personal relationships and 25–6
masks: identity as 9, 13
measurement 106–7, 107–11

media: as aid to day-dreaming 13; panics in 90, 91
men: identity 9; mother–child tie 51; part-time work 67; personal relationships 25–6
mental health service: preventative detention 94
middle class: friends 34, 46; moral beliefs 100; social capital 50; work 81–3
Milgram, Stanley: obedience to authority 121–2
military power: rationalization of 113
*Minority Report* (film) 94
mobility: job 67; of poverty 77; social 86–7
money: as measuring device 109–11
moral baggage 103
moral beliefs 100; context-dependent 100; failure of 98
moral entrepreneurs 91
moral panics 90–1
morality: rationalization and 115–19; sociology and 124
mothers: contact with 51; mother–child tie 42–3, 51
musicians: authenticity 14; study 7–8, 11

names: sense of belonging 11
nationalism 17–18
nationality: identity and 12–13
natural: assumptions as 10, 120–1; discipline of 117–19
negotiation: identity 9
neighbours 41; as distinct from friends 46; relationships with 43–7, 54; in United States 52, 53
networks, social 38–50; decline in 50–4
nicknames 11
*North by Northwest* (film) 96
nose blowing 118

obedience: to authority 121–2
obligation: family 102–4; gift exchange 102

occupations *see* work
old boy network 81
old people: care of 39, 52, 102; friends 34, 46; moral panics 91; neighbours 34, 46; personal networks 50, 51–2; single households 28
*One Foot in the Grave* (television series) 45
opportunity: inequality of 85–8, 88
order, social 39–40; coercion 92–8; exchange 101–5; problem of 89–92; values 98–100
organizations, social 47–50

panics 89–90; moral 90–1
parent–child tie 42–3, 51
parenting 31
part-time work 67
partnerships: intimacy and 27–9; *see also* marriage
peer groups: adolescent 100
performances: identity as 9; relationships as 23
personal networks: United States 52–3
personal relationships: eighteenth and early nineteenth centuries 23–4; at work 60–1; *see also* intimacy
personalities: rationalized 121
personality disorders: preventative detention 94
planning 106–7
political participation: United States 52
politicians: relationship with public 23
postmaterialist hypothesis 35–6
poverty 88; inequality and 75, 76–8; unemployment and 57–8
power 80
prestige 80; hierarchy of 4–5, 13–14; upper class 74, 81
prevention: of offending 93–4
prisons 92–3; limitations of coercion 95–6
privatism: family 29–33, 38–9, 45
production lines 113
provinces: everyday life 2

psychological factors: health 78
public events, great: effects of 2–3
punishment 92–4, 114–15
punks 11, 13–14

railways: timetables 108
rationalization 106–19; defined 107;
  as natural 121
reality: everyday life and 4
reciprocity 104; in families 103; gift
  exchanges 102; in prisons 96; in
  social events 41
reflexivity 20, 35
religion: difference and 16–17;
  privatization of 40; promotion of
  social cohesion 39–40; in United
  States 52; world-affirming and
  world-accommodating 15 16
religious people: moral beliefs 100
repetitive strain injury 69
reputation: moral identities 103–4
resilience, worker 70
resistance: at work 61–3, 114
restaurants 64
rite of passage: coming of age 18
routine work 59
routines: everyday life 2–3
rules 118–19; in bureaucracy 58–60
rumour 15
rural areas: community in 44

sabotage: at work 62, 95
satisfaction, job 68–9
scale: division of labour 112
science: rationalization 117
security: everyday life as source of 3
segregation, social 73
self: love 34–6; trajectory of 20
self-employment 67, 82
self-esteem 7
self-help groups 53
service class 82; social mobility 86–7
service sector 83; dismissive attitudes
  to clients 7; shift from
  manufacturing to 63–5
sexuality: male, and personal
  relationships 25–6

shame 15, 94
Shawshank Redemption, The (film)
  93
signals: identity 11–12
single households: growth of 28;
  reasons for 36
slavery 79
smiles 110–11
Smith, Adam: division of labour 112;
  markets 104
social capital see capital
social class see class
social order see order
socialization: primary 99; process of
  99–100; secondary 99
societies, leisure 48–9
sociology: examination of basic
  assumptions 3–5, 120–4
specialization: medical 112, 113–14;
  work 59, 112–13
spectators: in social groups 14
spitting 118
sports: rules 118; see also football
state see government policies
step-families 43
stereotypes: gender 10; identity and
  16–17
stoicism: replaced by emotional
  suffering 70
strangers: relationships with 24
stratification, social 73, 79–80; see
  also class, social
stress: work 68, 69–70
strikes 61–2, 95
subcontracting 67
suburbs: community in 45, 53
suffering, emotional 70
suicide: as index of social
  breakdown 39; personal
  relationships and 54
support see care
surveillance 114–15
surveillance society 94
symbols: sense of belonging 12

taboos 15; caste system 79
task-orientated societies 108

taxes: effect on income inequalities 74–5
teams, work 65–6, 68
telephone communication 53
television: fan clubs 49–50; as leisure pursuit 32–3, 53; relationship with viewers 23; time and 108–9
time: measurement of 108–9; work and 56–7
timetables 108, 114–15
Titmuss, Richard 101–2
Tolkien, J. R. R.: Lord of the Rings, The 117
trade unions 61–2
trust: intimacy and 24; nature of 104

underclass 77, 84
unemployment: experience of 57–8; rate of 67; sociological research on 5
uniforms 11
United States: blood transfusion service 101–2; informal work culture 60–1; life expectancy 78; personal networks 52–3; race 123; underclass 84
upper class 80; described 81; prestige of 74
urban areas: community in 44–5

values, common 98–100
victim: claim to status of 70
voluntary organizations 39, 41, 54; middle class in 50; social relationships and 47–9; United States 52

Wall Street (film) 63
wealth: beauty connected with 73; inequalities of 76

When Harry Met Sally (film) 22
women: changing roles of 10; friends 34; inequality 74; marriage 25, 27; personal relationships 25, 26; relationship with relatives 51; working-class 26, 84–5; see also mothers; work, women's
work: changes in 63–71; control at 94; described 56–8; division of labour 111–14; effect on personal relationships 53; effect on wider family relationships 42; at home 67; hours of 68–9; inequality in 74, 75–6; intensification of 68; organization of 58–63, 65–6; paid 56; part-time 67; social class and 80–5; social construction of 56; social contacts 41; unpredictable 66; in United States 52
work, women's 91; effect on personal relationships 51, 53; part-time 67
work cultures: informal 60–1, 62–3; sense of belonging 11–12
work patterns: changes in 56–7
working class: communities 44; friends 34, 46, 50; moral beliefs 100; romance 26; social mobility 86–7; work 83–5
Working Girl (film) 63
working to rule 60

young people: moral beliefs 100; peer groups 100; social situation 19–20; work 67
youth cultures: identity 11, 13–14; impact of social change on 19–20
youth unemployment 57